Kendall M. Weeker

Israel

ISRAEL

At the Center of History
& Revelation

Charles L. Feinberg

MULTNOMAH PRESS
PORTLAND. OREGON 97266

In loving memory of
A. E. P.
to whom I owe an eternal debt
and to
Miss Jessie H. Hunt
Kenneth Borden Jacques, M.D.
all lovers of God's beloved people Israel
this volume is affectionately
and gratefully dedicated

Cover design by Britt Taylor Collins

Third Edition

First Printing, 1980

Library of Congress Cataloging Publication Data

Feinberg, Charles Lee.
  Israel at the center of history & revelation

  Previous editions published under title Israel in the spotlight
  Includes index.
    1. Bible—Prophecies—Jews—Addresses, essays lectures I Title
BS649.J5F37   1980   220 1 5   80-12894
ISBN 0-930014-38-3

Printed in the United States of America

Contents

Foreword

ANYTHING WRITTEN TODAY concerning the Jewish nation is significant. But when a book appears from the pen of a scholar such as Dr. Charles L. Feinberg it becomes most significant indeed. I have read the manuscript with great interest and profit to my own heart and mind. This book is at once both informative and inspirational. It is the kind of book that one will not only enjoy reading through the first time, but will pick up again and again in order to obtain desired information on many phases of Bible truth.

As Dean and Professor of Semitics and Old Testament at Talbot Theological Seminary, Dr. Feinberg has presented portions of the contents of this book to the students in various courses which he teaches. They also have been a part of popular lectures which he has delivered throughout the country. They have appeared, in part, in the Dallas Theological Seminary's *Bibliotheca Sacra*. Some of these chapters have been given as addresses at the Jewish meetings in the Church of the Open Door, Los Angeles. In view of the wide variety of audiences and the many areas in which these messages have been given, and the great blessing which has always attended their presentation, it is evident that they are meeting a real need in the minds of Christian people everywhere.

It is expected that this book will have a wide acceptance. It will stir much thought on the part of readers. It will send

7

students of the Word back to their Bibles to review portions of the Old Testament. It will explain hitherto obscure passages and will open to the mind of the careful reader many new avenues of study in God's holy Word.

Dr. Feinberg is a brother greatly beloved in the Lord. He has unusual intellectual capacity, coupled with a depth of spiritual insight, which marks him as one of the outstanding biblical, and especially Old Testament, scholars in the country today. His classroom work is extremely thorough, and students whom he teaches emerge with a thorough and comprehensive knowledge of the subject. We of the Bible Institute of Los Angeles, Inc., are looking forward to the privilege of having many more publications come from Dr. Feinberg's mind and heart. The great body of Christian literature is being, and will yet be, greatly enriched by his written ministry.

LOUIS T. TALBOT

Preface

SINCE THE FIRST DAY that my redeemed heart read the words of the Lord Jesus Christ: *"'O Jerusalem, Jerusalem, who kills the prophets and stones those who are sent to her! How often I wanted to gather your children together, the way a hen gathers her chicks under her wings, and you were unwilling,'"* (Matthew 23:37), the poignant and throbbing heart of the Saviour was laid bare in an unforgettable manner. In that hour I caught a glimpse of the overwhelming love of the Lord which has remained with me through the years. It is basic to the understanding of the Word of God to see clearly the place of Israel, the world, and the Church in the plan of God. But coupled with this grasp of the material, there must be a Spirit-imparted love for every segment of the human family. Among the souls for whom Christ died are multitudes in Israel, and I seek to reemphasize scriptural love for them, those who are truly "beloved for the fathers' sake."

Israel is unquestionably coming more and more into the arena of world events. If we read the prophetic Scriptures aright, this trend is due to increase rapidly as the world nears its fateful and cataclysmic denouement. As the child of God views the people of Israel drawn more and more into the very vortex of global affairs, he may be assured that the hour of the Church's redemption draws on apace. God has more than once in His Word indicated time elements with regard to Israel (their Egyptian bondage, the Babylonian Captivity, the

9

seventy weeks of Daniel 9), and as we study the timepiece of
God, we shall know where we are in God's dealings and how
we are to conduct ourselves in these last days of a fast dying
age.

The following pages have been written in the midst of a
busy ministry of teaching, preaching, and administration.
Many have been the expressions of blessing received through
those portions which have been delivered as messages in Bible
conferences, church services, and radio broadcasting. It is
because of this encouragement and repeated requests that I
have felt constrained to put the material in book form. In
some of the sections the personal note is retained purposely,
so that the Spirit of God may use the words unto salvation,
should the eye of an unbelieving Jew or Gentile fall upon
them.

Grateful thanks are here extended to the Dallas Theological Seminary for permission to use both unpublished mater-
ials, as well as writings which have appeared over a number of
years in *Bibliotheca Sacra*, their theological quarterly. Illus-
trations of Bible truth have been gleaned from a wide area,
and we express our indebtedness and thanks to many writers.
For help on the manuscript rendered by my wife, my son
Paul, and my daughter Lois, appreciation is here expressed.

May the triune God, who loves Israel with an everlasting
love, be magnified through these pages, and may the Spirit of
God lead souls to the Saviour through the renewed vision and
zeal of many of God's children.

Part 1

ISRAEL IN THE LAW

1

The Conflict of Isaac and Ishmael

"Tell me, you who want to be under the law, do you not listen to the law? For it is written that Abraham had two sons, one by the bondwoman and one by the free woman. But the son by the bondwoman was born according to the flesh, and the son by the free woman through the promise. This contains an allegory: for these women are two covenants, one proceeding from Mount Sinai bearing children who are to be slaves; she is Hagar. Now this Hagar is Mount Sinai in Arabia, and corresponds to the present Jerusalem, for she is in slavery with her children. But the Jerusalem above is free; she is our mother. For it is written, 'Rejoice, barren woman who does not bear; break forth and shout, you who are not in labor; for more are the children of the desolate than of the one who has a husband.' And you brethren, like Isaac, are children of promise. But as at that time he who was born according to the flesh persecuted him who was born according to the Spirit, so it is now also. But what does the Scripture say? 'Cast out the bondwoman and her son, for the son of the bondwoman shall not be an heir with the son of the free woman.' So then, brethren, we are not children of a bondwoman, but of the free woman."

(Galatians 4:21-31)

INTRODUCTION

IT IS A SETTLED and assured biblical principle, well known to
students of the Scriptures, that certain past events project
themselves into the future and form the pattern and mold for
prophetic events. Such an example is to be found in the Exodus of the people of Israel from Egyptian bondage. In
chapter 11 of his prophecy, Isaiah foretells how in a coming
day God will regather His scattered and dispersed people
from Assyria, Egypt, Pathros, Cush, Elam, Shinar, Hamath,
and the islands of the sea. Then he notes that God will utterly
dry up the tongue of the Egyptian sea (as He dried up the Red
Sea of old), so that the returning remnant could march over
dry shod.

And there will be a highway for the restored exiles from
Assyria *"just as there was for Israel in the day that they came
up out of the land of Egypt"* (Isaiah 11:11-16; see Jeremiah
23:1-8). What God has done in the past is held out as an indication of what He will yet do in and for Israel. Take, for instance, the events in the life of the patriarch Jacob as related
to the land of Canaan. He was settled in the land, through the
anger of Esau he had to flee the land to Mesopotamia, and
then he returned to the land. This is a pattern of his descendants, Israel, who lived in the land for centuries, have been
exiled these many centuries from the land, and will yet be
restored to their own land. After this manner Isaac and
Ishmael form a pattern, too.

THE PARENTAGE OF ISHMAEL AND ISAAC

Because Ishmael and Isaac had the same father, it is not to
be inferred that they were similar in every respect. From a
comparison of Genesis 13:1-2 with 16:1 we note that
Abraham (Abram) brought two things with him from Egypt:
(1) wealth and (2) an Egyptian handmaid, Hagar. What trouble, strife, separation, and conflict were caused by the wealth
from Egypt is clearly shown in chapters 13 to 15. Chapters 16
and following reveal what discord was introduced through

the bringing of Hagar into the homelife of Abraham and Sarah. Ishmael, child of Hagar, came ultimately from Egypt, which is a "type" of the world and all that is opposed to God (see Revelation 11:8). Egypt stands as the great oppressor of the people of God, just as the world would enslave God's own in every age. Moreover, Ishmael was from the flesh (Galatians 4:23, 29).

When Abraham and Sarah would not abide God's time for the promised child, the man of faith hearkened to the fleshly arrangements of his wife in order to have a child by his handmaid. And from this union have come those who have been the inveterate enemies of the Gospel of Christ through the centuries, namely, the seed of Ishmael. Esau also represents in the Scriptures the flesh and its desires. When we turn to Genesis 36:3 for the list of the wives of Esau, we are not at all surprised to find that one of them is *"Basemath, Ishmael's daughter, the sister of Nebaioth."* The flesh is joined to the flesh; flesh ever gravitates to its own level, the flesh. Finally, when we seek the origins of Ishmael we must recall that he is from unbelief also. Despite the clear promises of God, Abraham prayed earnestly, *"Oh that Ishmael might live before Thee!"* This was unmitigated unbelief. To this supplication God answered, *"No!"* (Cf. Genesis 17:18-19). Such is the background of the life of Ishmael.

Isaac, on the other hand, was the child of promise. Read the record: *"But God said, 'No, but Sarah your wife shall bear you a son, and you shall call his name Isaac; and I will establish My covenant with him for an everlasting covenant for his descendants after him'"* (Genesis 17:19). Paul states clearly that *"the son by the free woman [was born] through the promise"* (Galatians 4:23). Isaac was the seed of the coming Messiah in whom all God's redemptive purposes were and are centered. The promise stated that *"'in you all the families of the earth shall be blessed'"* (Genesis 12:3). That this definitely predicted the Messiah, the Lord Jesus Christ, is confirmed by the word of the Holy Spirit through the apostle Paul: *"Now the promises were spoken to Abraham and to his seed. He does not say, 'And to seeds,' as referring to many, but rather to one, 'And to your seed,' that is, Christ"* (Galatians 3:16).

And this promise included Isaac, because the genealogy in the Gospel of Matthew (1:2) and that in the Gospel of Luke (3:34) both incorporate the name of Isaac in the honored lineage of the Messiah of Israel.

Moreover, to Isaac was given the land of promise with all the blessings attendant upon occupation therein. Note Genesis 12:7 and 13:14-17, two of many passages that record promises concerning the land. Notice the recurring words of importance: "land" and "seed." Isaac was the child of promise and by virtue of that was related to all the blessings in the land of promise. Put it down as an incontrovertible fact of the Bible that the land of promise and the seed of promise are not to be separated for all time. They are inseparably linked.

At this point one may be inclined to ask, Why, then, was Ishmael the firstborn? The Bible principle is that the natural always comes first and is superseded by the spiritual. First it is the natural Adam, then last it is the spiritual Adam; first Ishmael, then Isaac; first Esau, then Jacob; first the natural birth, then the spiritual birth; first the natural body in this life, then the spiritual body in the resurrection (1 Corinthians 15:44). The natural seed, as Ishmael, is always motivated by unbelief.

A friend once said to Dr. Agnew Johnson, "It will be ten thousand years before India becomes Christian."

"You are drawing a hard line on God," said the doctor.

"Oh, I forgot about Him," was the startling reply.

"Then," said the doctor, "you can make it ten million years if you leave Him out." Unbelief never reckons on the power and promise of the living God.

THE PORTION OF ISHMAEL AND ISAAC

What portion was allotted to these respective children of Abraham? With respect to Ishmael, God had promised:

"'And as for Ishmael, I have heard you; behold, I will bless him, and will make him fruitful, and will multiply him exceedingly. He shall become the father of twelve princes, and I will make him a great nation'" (Genesis 17:20). A great people and nation are promised to Ishmael. Indeed, the peoples that have come from Ishmael are fruitful and populous.

A further word was spoken concerning this son: *"'And he will be a wild donkey of a man, his hand will be against everyone, and everyone's hand will be against him; and he will live to the east of all his brothers'"* (Genesis 16:12). This passage is full of light on Ishmael and contains certain important details. Ishmael as a wild donkey among men would be of unbridled and unrestrained nature. His would be a rough and raw existence. Just as the wild donkey makes his home in the desert (Job 39:5-8), so the sons of Ishmael have been known as the sons of the desert. Furthermore, he would be at sword's point with all men; and all men would be in conflict with him. He would be a hostile and belligerent nation. And he was to dwell east (see Genesis 25:18) of his brethren, where his stronghold has been ever since that time.

The portion of Isaac was a blessed one, as has been touched upon in part already. He was in the line of promise with all the spiritual blessings promised Abraham descending directly to him (Genesis 12:1-3; 15:12-21, the exact title deed to the land in perpetuity; 22:15-18, the confirmation of the covenant blessings after the offering up of Isaac in intent; 26:1-5, the reaffirmation of all the promises to Isaac in a time of famine and need). Subsequent history shows Isaac was drawn to spiritualities. It is true that the experiences of Genesis 22 were meant to test and prove the faith of Abraham (verse 1), but Isaac was no inanimate object without thought or feeling during the tremendous events of that hour. He willingly submitted himself to the altar of sacrifice when he saw that preparation was being made to offer him.

The Scriptures pass over that phase in silence, it is true, but neither do they record any word of drawing back or rebellion on the part of Isaac. He definitely was mindful of the higher

things of life, the spiritual things. On the contrary, Ishmael
was always attracted to temporalities, and the things of time
and sense. When we read of Ishmaelites, they are merchants
going down to Egypt (see Genesis 37:25; 39:1). The world and
its interests loomed all important for Ishmael and his descendants. But with Isaac were the great and exceeding promises
of God which were and are of a world-comprehensive character. His was a blessed and full portion.

The Persecution of Isaac by Ishmael

If you should consider at this point that the word "persecution" is too strong a word, turn to Galatians 4:29 where you
will find the word "persecuted." It is the Holy Spirit's own
word. And the more one contemplates the details of the
biblical narrative in the Genesis chapters, the better he shall
comprehend the full meaning of the persecution indicated.

Just think back on the situation in the home of Abraham
with the elder son displaced from the heirship. In the Orient
this was no small matter. The firstborn was to have a double
portion of the inheritance. In this instance it belonged not to
Ishmael but Isaac. Would the natural man find any delight in
such an arrangement which set aside his fleshly claims? Then
pause for a moment to consider the contention in the home
which must have gone on between Hagar and Sarah.

It appears that the climax to all this conflict and dis-
harmony was reached at the weaning of Isaac (see Genesis
21:8-11). In the East this stage in the life of a child is reached
when he is between three and five years of age. It is a time of
particular joy because the early hardships and dangers of in-
fant life have been successfully passed. For that reason
Abraham made a joyous feast for his heir according to the
promise. It was more than Ishmael could down, and he made
a mockery of the whole affair. The patience of Sarah was exhausted, and she demanded the expulsion of the handmaid
and her son. Why is so much being made of a simple unhappy
home scene? Because the effects of it were never dissipated.

The book of Nehemiah, the account of the rebuilding of the walls of Jerusalem according to the will and purpose of God, lists the enemies of the work of God among His people (4:7-8). Among the antagonists of God's work were the Arabians, sons of Ishmael. Centuries later one of the most solemn scenes in all human history was transacted. The blessed Son of God, the incarnate Second Person of the Trinity, was on trial for His life before none other than Herod. And who was his ancestor, Herod the Great, as to parentage? Mark this: his mother was a Nabataean (of Ishmael) and his father was of Idumaean (Esau) extraction). The Son of Isaac was being judged by the son of Ishmael.

What has been the attitude of Ishmael's seed toward Isaac's seed through the years? The psalmist gives the whole picture:

"O God, do not remain quiet;
Do not be silent, and, O God, do not be still.
For, behold, Thine enemies make an uproar;
And those who hate Thee have exalted themselves.
They make shrewd plans against Thy people,
And conspire together against Thy treasured ones.
They have said, 'Come, and let us wipe them out as
    a nation;
That the name of Israel be remembered no more.'
For they have conspired together with one mind;
Against Thee do they make a covenant:
The tents of Edom and the Ishmaelites [note the
    placement of these names at the head of the list];
Moab, and the Hagrites;
Gebal, and Ammon, and Amalek;
Philistia with the inhabitants of Tyre;
Assyria also has joined with them;
They have become a help to the children of Lot."

(Psalm 83:1-8)

Nothing less than the complete extinction and annihilation of God's people, Israel, have been the goal and aim of the

Ishmaelites through the course of their history. During the Middle Ages the sons of Ishmael (the Arabs) subjugated large portions of Europe and the countries to the east, thus aiding the Romish Church to make those ages the Dark Ages of history. And today these sons of Ishmael are among the greatest adversaries of the Gospel of our own blessed Lord and Saviour, Jesus Christ.

And what of Ishmael in the twentieth century, since we would bring the story down to our own day? We have all read of the conflict carried on and the bloodshed in the 1929 riots in Palestine. After 1929, when the first serious outbreaks took place, the Arab leaders' fears of losing their positions, a developing nationalism among younger Arabs, administrative problems and bunglings of the British civil administration in Palestine, and the propaganda of Fascists and Nazis in Europe combined to set the stage for constant tension, riot, and civil war. From 1936 to 1939 a minor rebellion dragged on. The British Peel Report of 1937 advocated partition of the land into Arab, Jewish, and British states. The solution, though disappointing to the Jews, was accepted by them as a first step toward a better arrangement later. The Arabs refused to negotiate and started the worst disturbances to that time in Palestine.

In May 1939, the Chamberlain government issued its famous White Paper, scrapping the Balfour Declaration. Only another 70,000 Jews were to be admitted in the next five years with Palestine's final status to be an independent state with two Arabs to every Jew.[1]

Early in 1947 the British Labour Government decided Palestine was too heavy a burden and announced its intention to surrender the Mandate. By November 29 the United Nations authorized the partition of Palestine into independent Arab and Jewish states. Arab guerrillas and mercenaries soon struck in different parts of the country. When the British withdrawal was accomplished and the new State of Israel was

---

[1] A. L. Sachar, *A History of the Jews* (New York: 1967), pp. 405 ff.

declared on May 14, 1948, seven Arab states openly marshaled their armies to fight the partition.

On June 11 the United Nations imposed a truce of four weeks. Arabs struck again on July 9, but after about a week the Israeli victory was a devastating one. A second truce followed. A third round in the war convinced the Arabs that the Israelis could not be dislodged from the land. An armistice was signed on February 24, 1949, between Israel and Egypt. By July 20 all the Arab states had signed the armistice.

But the conflict did not end there. In October of 1956, Israel (with England and France) attacked Egyptian guerrilla bases and troop concentrations in the Sinai in order to clear them. This confrontation resulted in an uneasy truce which lasted until June 1967. In May of that year Nasser of Egypt notified U Thant of the UN that he wanted the UN forces, stationed for ten years on the U.A.R.–Israeli border in the Gaza Strip and on the heights commanding the Strait of Tiran, removed in order to move Egyptian troops to face Israel. U Thant's answer was the UN forces would remain where they were or they would be withdrawn at once. Moreover, he offered that, if the U.A.R. government made a formal request to him for complete withdrawal of UN forces, he would comply immediately. The Six-Day War (June 5-10) followed with unprecedented victory for Israel. Jerusalem was taken and reunified on June 29.

The years following the 1967 conflict were difficult ones. Palestinian terrorist organizations took their toll of Israeli life and property. King Hussein of Jordan confronted the illegal fighters and overthrew them, ridding his realm of their presence. In 1971 Al-Fatah based its operations largely from Lebanon. This state of affairs could not continue indefinitely without outbreak of hostilities. Thus, on October 6, 1973 (Yom Kippur, the sacred Day of Atonement), new hostilities began, the Egyptians striking from the west and Syria from the northeast. This conflict lasted almost the remainder of the month.

In 1974 following negotiations by the U.S., Israel withdrew from the west bank of the Suez Canal. Another withdrawal was effected in 1976, granting the Egyptians territory and an oil field. Palestinian guerrilla warfare continues throughout the Middle East with constant preemptive and reprisal attacks from Israel. If in any sense this state of affairs can be considered peace, it is a very uneasy and shallow one. Further antagonism has resulted from the fact that by 1976, Arabs were able to have several (actually, a dozen) anti-Israel resolutions passed at the UN General Assembly, climaxing in the designation of Zionism as "a form of racism."

A brief look at 1977 figures for Israeli armed forces underlines Jewish designs for a free and independent Israel much more emphatically. Israel's regular army had a strength in 1977 of 138,000 (18,000 regulars) including 12,000 women. There was a reserve force of around 375,000 on mobilization. Naval personnel in 1977 totaled 350 officers and 4,150 men. Naval reserves were 5,000. The air force had a personnel strength amounting to about 21,000, with over 500 first-line aircraft, all jets.

The "peace initiative" in 1978 and 1979 took on more sober dimensions in view of the need for implementation.[2]

What are the events of our own day in Palestine if not a living prolongation of that struggle and conflict which went on in the home (in Palestine too) of Abraham in that century long ago? The reports that reach us weekly, even daily, confirm the presence of the age-long animosity between Isaac and Ishmael. Whether it be repeated incidents along the Israeli borders, the infiltration of Jordanians into the State of Israel, or the retaliations of the Israelis, we are reminded repeatedly, even incessantly, that the contention between the sons of Abraham is not yet at an end.

---

[2] For fuller details on these important areas see *The World Almanac*, 1979, pp. 547-549; *American Jewish Yearbook for 1977*, vol. 77, pp. 481, 489; John Paxton, ed., *The Statesman's Year-Book for 1978-1979*, pp. 706-714; *Encyclopedia Britannica, 1979 Book of the Year*, pp. 459-460.

And is this the conclusion of the matter? No, it is not! Just as Sarah of old commanded, *"'Drive out this maid and her son, for the son of this maid shall not be an heir with my son Isaac'"* (Genesis 21:10), so now the Spirit of God through Paul says, *"Cast out the bondwoman and her son, for the son of the bondwoman shall not be an heir with the son of the free woman"* (Galatians 4:30).

A word of caution is in order here. The Scripture is not to be interpreted as though the sons of Ishmael are not objects of the grace of God who can by faith receive eternal life on the sole basis of faith in the Lord Jesus Christ. God is not in this age dealing primarily with national entities in the area of salvation. Anywhere in the Bible salvation is always on an individual basis.

God will in His own time cast out the sons of Ishmael, despite their devisings and intrigues. And He will settle the sons of Isaac, in spite of their continual crying for help to the helpless nations of the earth instead of turning now to the Lord God who gave them the land forever—He will settle them in the land of promise in perpetuity.

OF WHAT GOOD IS THE LAND?

But at this point I would ask a pertinent question. Of what profit or avail is the land to Israel, the sons of Isaac, as long as they are lost, dead in trespasses and sins, not trusting in the Messiah and God of Abraham, Isaac, and Jacob? It is of no use to them as far as spiritual things are concerned. They must become sons of Isaac by faith as well as by birth. God has given us the privilege and opportunity of getting the Gospel to them. What will we do about it?

2

Blessing from the Jews

THE SECOND PROPHECY of the Messiah in the Old Testament is like the first, in that it is the utterance of a blessing in the midst of a curse. When Adam fell, God gave the first prophetic promise in Genesis 3:15 concerning the woman's seed and His victory over the serpent, Satan. When Noah fell, the prophecy was given in Genesis 9:25-27: *"So he said, 'Cursed be Canaan; a servant of servants he shall be to his brothers.' He also said, 'Blessed be the* LORD,[1] *the God of Shem; and let Canaan be his servant. May God enlarge Japeth, and let him dwell in the tents of Shem; and let Canaan be his servant.'"*

The occasion was the shame of Noah and the sin of Ham. Noah himself is the prophet, and in his prophecy he lays down the outlines of the moral character of the nations yet to be born from his sons: the sensual nature of Ham and his descendants which made them subservient, the ideal and broad nature of Japheth and his progeny, the spiritual nature of Shem and his offspring. Of Ham have come the servile peoples, the Phoenicians, Egyptians, Ethiopians, and Canaanites; of Japheth, the nations of influence in government, art, and the humanities; of Shem, the nations of religion. Almost all Jewish and Christian interpreters have seen in this passage a prophecy of the Messiah.

---

[1]The LORD is used in place of Jehovah from the New American Standard Bible.

Again, as indicated in the discussion previously, individual
destiny of the descendants of these nations is not involved.
Salvation is available to all the descendants of Noah based on
a personal acceptance of the Saviour. Refer, for example, to
Acts 8:25 ff, the case of the Ethiopian eunuch, and to Acts
13:1, the case of Simeon called Niger.

In treating this passage with special reference to Shem we
see three great truths. In the first place, there is indicated the
repository of the truth.

THE REPOSITORY OF THE TRUTH

When God is designated as the "God of Shem" it is the first
place in Scripture where God is called the God of any individual. It denotes a peculiar relationship and signifies that
God has entered into a vital and spiritual bond with this individual. There has been a definite choice, and it is God's purpose to use such a one to His glory. From this time on, Shem
was the center of biblical and redemptive history. God would
use him for the channel of the Messiah and the salvation of
man. How can we explain God's choice of Shem over his two
brothers? The love of God alone can explain His choice of
any individual, and account for His making Shem the repository or preserver of the truth.

Two men were riding together. As they were about to separate, one of them said to the other: "Do you ever read your
Bible?"

"Yes, but I get no benefit from it, because, to tell you the
truth, I feel that I do not love God."

"Neither did I," said the other, "but I found from the Bible
that God loved me. And He loves you, too, my friend." This
was something that man had never thought of before. He
began to read the Bible as he had never read it before.
Though it is written so plainly in the Scriptures, men still
marvel at and will not accept the truth of God's love. Yet it
was this love which touched Shem to make his life a channel
for spiritual truth and blessing.

The prophecy of Noah points out, in the second place, the revealer of the truth.

THE REVEALER OF THE TRUTH

In this seed of all future prophecy which contains practically the prophetic history of the world, the emphasis is on Japheth and even more so on Shem. The blessing of Japheth is twofold: (1) expansion and extension over a wide area, (2) dwelling in the tents of Shem. Japheth's expansion is seen in the list of the nations in Genesis 10:2-5. The territorial expansion of the Japhetic peoples is well known. They gained the north of western Asia, a large part of the interior area, and all of Europe. They have the colonizing spirit coupled with extensive migrations. Political and commercial progress and activity are in view here as well. Japheth, extending from India across Europe and the Western Hemisphere, has been the world's colonizer and populator. But spiritually, down through the centuries, the Japhethites have been and still are indebted to the descendants of Shem.

Follow the line of fulfillment in Genesis 12:3 (*"all the families of the earth"*); 49:10 (*"of the peoples"*); John 4:22 and Romans 3:1-2 (the Scriptures); 9:4-5 (the promises, the covenants, and the Messiah); Romans 11 (grafted into the good olive tree); Ephesians 3:1-10 (true even for this age as fellow heirs, fellow members, and fellow partakers in the Gospel); Zechariah 8:23 (the nations led to the worship of God through the Jews); Isaiah 2:2-4 (millennial blessing through Jerusalem and the Jews). The language of the New Testament is Japheth (Greek) dwelling in the tents of Shem. Gentile believers are for the most part the descendants of Japheth dwelling in the tents of Shem. Japhethites have entered into the religious riches and privileges of Shem. Japheth is Shem's guest. The God, the Bible, the Saviour, the salvation that the world enjoys, are from Shem through the Jew. How great is our debt to the Jew!

"Nothing Jewish in my house!" These were the words of a wealthy man who was entertaining a well-known minister. Said he, "I have such a hatred for the Jew that I will have nothing Jewish in my house." The minister quietly arose and took a beautifully bound Bible from the table and a New Testament from the bookcase and put them before the fireplace. He then went on to take down some paintings from the wall. He removed one picture of Paul preaching at Athens and another of the crucifixion. The man was greatly surprised and asked, "What are you doing? Why are you taking such liberties in my house?"

To this the minister answered, "You just said that you would not have anything Jewish in your house. I was beginning to help you to take away the many Jewish things you happen to have in this room. Shall I throw them into the fire?"

"Stop! Stop!" the man cried. "May God forgive me. I have never thought of it in that light. Little did I know how greatly indebted I was to things Jewish." Too many Gentile believers have failed to realize in whose spiritual tents they are living!

In the last place, our passage points out vividly enough our responsibility to the truth.

OUR RESPONSIBILITY TO THE TRUTH

Once we realize how fully we have entered into the spiritual blessing of the Jew, will we not take to heart the words of the Scriptures? They tell us that the Gospel of Christ is the power of God unto salvation to everyone that believeth, to the Jew first, and also to the Gentile. They remind us that Gentile followers of the Jewish Messiah are indebted to Israel as partakers of their spiritual things (Romans 1:16; 15:27). They indicate that the Gospel, the message of Good News, is to be preached for the remission of sins from Jerusalem to all peoples. They outline God's strategy in the world spread of the truth by beginning at Jerusalem and reaching out to the uttermost part of the earth. How can we manifest gratitude for dwelling in the tents of Shem and never tell Israel of their spiritual riches in the Messiah, the Lord Jesus Christ? We have this God-given responsibility and opportunity; let us avail ourselves of it. When this is done, God is mightily glorified.

A Mr. Reichart, a missionary to the Jews in Cairo, Egypt, acted as the depository of the British Bible Society. In his store one day, he had a visit from a small party of Arabian Jews. They had heard somehow of the shop in Cairo and they came for Hebrew Old Testaments. Reichart very gladly supplied them; but before he closed the box, with earnest prayer and without a word, he put in a Hebrew New Testament, hidden with the Old. The Arabian Jews went away, and then in a year or two some men came back again, bringing a letter. This letter stated how highly Mr. Reichart's first visitors valued the beautiful copies of the Law, Prophets, and Psalms, and also how surprised they were to find another book in the holy tongue, about which they had never known. The Person of whom it spoke had never crossed their knowledge before, and as they read of Him in the holy words of the book, enclosed with their Scriptures, with one mind they had come to the conclusion that He was Israel's Messiah. This was a blessed way in which to fulfill the responsibility for dwelling in Shem's tents.

Christian friend, from the very moment you trusted Christ as Saviour and Lord, you began to dwell in the tents of Shem. How long has it been since you have paid your tent rent? Have you ever paid it? Have you ever told a Jewish soul about his Messiah and Saviour?

Part 2

ISRAEL IN THE PROPHETS

3

A Chaotic Future
Without the Messiah

MANY ARE THE WOULD-BE EXPERTS today who think they can look into the future and outline for us precisely the turn of events. It is well that these pronouncements are forgotten as soon as they are made or shortly thereafter, or only embarrassment would result from a comparison of them with the actual manner in which events do transpire. In short, only God has the power to look into the future and tell us what will come to pass. He knows the end from the beginning, so both alike are clear to Him. He has graciously sketched for us the trend of world events in a number of portions of Scripture.

A remarkable instance is to be found in the book of Ezekiel. The prophet Ezekiel was one of the captivity prophets who not only saw the kingdom of Judah go into Babylonian captivity, but was exiled there himself. We find him at the outset of his prophecy among the captives by the river Chebar (1:1). His messages are largely those of judgment, as are those of Jeremiah, because the people of God in that day were ripe for judgment. But like all the prophets, he has God's remedy for the disaster that Israel has brought upon itself.

The unusual passage which pictures for us the program of events for the future is found in chapter 21:24-27, where the prophet declares: *"Therefore, thus says the Lord God, 'Because you have made your iniquity to be remembered, in that your transgressions are uncovered, so that in all your deeds your sins appear—because you have come to remembrance, you will be seized with the hand. And you, O slain, wicked one, the prince of Israel, whose day has come, in the time of punishment of the end,' thus says the Lord God, 'Remove the turban and take off the crown; this will be no more the same. Exalt that which is low, and abase that which is high. A ruin, a ruin, a ruin, I shall make it. This also will be no more, until He comes whose right it is; and I shall give it to Him.'"*

There are three striking truths in this portion of the prophecy of Ezekiel. The first is the cause of the judgment.

THE CAUSE OF THE JUDGMENT

There are three principal prophecies of judgment in chapter 21: (1) against the whole land of Israel (vv. 2-3 ff.); (2) against King Zedekiah, the last king of Judah (v. 25); and (3) against the land of Ammon (v. 28). The Lord's sharpened sword is in prominence and devours on every hand. This sword is mentioned fifteen times. It is drawn from its sheath, it is sharpened for slaughter, and it is furbished to make it as lightning. The cause of the judgment on Israel is distinctly stated. They have made their iniquities so memorable, and their transgressions have been so flagrant and outbroken, that their sins are manifest in all their deeds. They have heaped unto themselves iniquity and transgression and sin until they are ensnared in their own inevitable noose.

And the weak and wicked King Zedekiah was the very symbol of the sin of the nation. He is addressed in most severe terms: *"'You, O slain, wicked one, the prince of Israel'"* (21:25), as though he were already suffering the dire punishment which his sins have brought upon him. The language is most vivid and emphatic. The hour of his judgment has come. How completely this was carried out is known from the fact of his deportation to Babylon, the slaying of his sons before his eyes, and then the putting out of his eyes by the cruel enemy. The white light of God's Word lays bare every sinful thing; it did in the case of Zedekiah and all Israel, and it does so for everyone now.

Some years ago when modern chemistry was in its early growth, a fashionable audience gathered in Paris for an experimental lecture on chemistry. When they came out into the open, they greeted one another with exclamations of dismay. The faces of most of the women had been ludicrously transformed. Their cheeks, lips, and in some cases the entire surface of exposed skin had turned into varying shades of blue, yellow, or violet. The chemical effects of the gases released during the lecture had touched everyone who had used any cosmetics. When the piercing light of God's presence and Word shines into the hearts of men, everything that has been hidden becomes open, and the naked things are made manifest.

The second arresting truth in our Scripture is the chaos predicted.

THE CHAOS PREDICTED

The judgment on Zedekiah was only the beginning of woe for Israel. The prophet Ezekiel foretells that chaos will result from the judgment that God brings. All will be turned upside down. The turban of the high priest would be gone, the crown from the head of the king of Israel would be removed, the low would be exalted, and the high would be brought low. As clearly as words can tell, it is stated that society would be in a state of revolution, commotion, and upheaval. This passage is the death sentence on the Aaronic priesthood and the Davidic monarchy in the form in which it had existed.

The prophet predicts the complete overthrow of both offices. When Judah was led captive to Babylon, it marked the end of the rule by the kings of David's dynasty. Also, the Ark and the Shekinah glory were not present in the Temple of Zerubbabel, nor were the Urim and Thummim (Ezra 2:63). Overturning is to be the order of the day. Ezekiel says, "This not [shall not be] this," that is, nothing will be allowed to remain as it had been before. Revolution and upheaval will be the order of the day. Everything from the lowest to the highest will be turned upside down. There will be rest and security nowhere. And this appeared so, not only for Israel but with the kingdoms and empires that followed: Babylon, Medo-Persia, Greece, and Rome.

In more recent times we have witnessed the loss of rule by many crowned heads of the world, and the exaltation to office of the base. When we think of the European scene—although it is true universally—during the past dozen and more years, we are made to realize as never before the aptness of Ezekiel's prophecy; we have witnessed gangsterism on an international level. And the end is not yet. Men have turned things upside down all too often, and now it is God's turn to do so. World chaos has been brought about by the judgment of God. There is no peace nor security.

Spurgeon, the great English preacher, once said that wise men of old claimed that no sin was ever committed whose consequences rested on the head of the sinner alone. No man can do ill and his fellows not suffer. He illustrated it in this way: a vessel from Joppa carried a passenger one day who, beneath his berth, cut a hole through the ship's side. When the men on watch reasoned with him, "What are you doing, O miserable man?" the offender said calmly, "What matters it to you? The hole I have made lies under my own berth!" When God began to overturn in Israel, there was upheaval and has been everywhere ever since.

But our portion of the Word of God indicates, in the last place, the coming of the peace-bringer.

THE COMING OF THE PEACE-BRINGER

God assures us that this overturning will not go on endlessly. There will be a limit and an end to the chaos. It will terminate with the coming of the One whose right it is to rule and reign. All men are ultimately incompetent to wield and hold authority. There is One, however, who has this right, and it is Shiloh of Judah's tribe and the King from the line of David. The words "until he comes" are an allusion to the prophecy in Genesis 49:10: *"The scepter shall not depart from Judah, nor the ruler's staff* [a lawgiver] *from between his feet, until Shiloh comes, and to him shall be the obedience of the peoples.'"* The empty throne is waiting for the coming of the rightful Occupant. The right to the priesthood and the throne are the Messiah's.

Zechariah foretold, *"'It is He who will build the temple of the* LORD, *and He who will bear the honor, and sit and rule on His throne. Thus, He will be a priest on His throne'"* (6:13). Here are royalty and priesthood united and blended in one glorious Person, that of the Messiah and Saviour of Israel, the Lord Jesus Christ. David was prophesying of Him too when he spoke in Psalm 110 of the Messiah as ruling in the midst of His enemies, and at the same time fulfilling the high priesthood after the order of Melchizedek.

The angel Gabriel announced that the Lord God would give the Messiah the throne of His father David, and He would rule over the house of Jacob forever, and of His kingdom there would be no end (Luke 1:32-33). In the Tractate Sota of the Talmud it is said: "The Urim and Thummim, and the king from David's stem, had ceased with the destruction, and their restoration is to be expected only when the dead are raised up, and the Messiah, David's Son, appears." Chaos— note it carefully—can only cease when the Messiah of God appears.

At a missionary meeting on the island of Raratonga in the Pacific Ocean, an old man arose and said, "I have lived during the reign of four kings. In the first we were continually at war, and a fearful season it was. During the second we were overtaken with a severe famine, and then we ate rats and grass and wood. During the third we were conquered and became the peck and prey of the two other settlements of the island. But during the reign of this third king, we were visited by another King, a great King, a good King, a peaceful King, a King of love, Jesus, the Lord from heaven. He has gained the victory. He has conquered our hearts; therefore, we now have peace of heart and soul in this world, and hope soon to dwell with Him in Heaven." Only the peace-bringer can accomplish this.

Do not be misled into thinking that conditions will be otherwise than given in God's Word. Israel without her King is in unrest, in famine for the Word of the Lord, and at the mercy of many enemies the world over. Let her trust in God the Messiah and know peace and security. To you, the individual Jew, as well as Gentile, who is out of Christ, who has never trusted Him for salvation, there is chaos, unrest, turmoil, and strife in your heart and will continue to be until Messiah the Saviour is given His rightful place and sway. Turn your heart to Him now!

4

Israel, the Apple of God's Eye

ZECHARIAH was one of the prophets who lived after the Babylonian captivity in the time of the restoration of Israel to their own land. He had a message of spiritual importance for the remnant of God's people who returned to Palestine. He also warned those who were remaining in Babylon of the coming judgment upon all those nations who had afflicted God's people, Israel. In the midst of this prophecy he stated that those who touch Israel, the Jew, touch the apple of God's eye. Zechariah declared: *"For thus says the LORD of hosts, 'After glory He has sent me against the nations which plunder you, for he who touches you, touches the apple of His eye'"* (2:8). There are three expressions in the Old Testament translated "apple of the eye."

In Deuteronomy 32:10, Moses describes God's loving care of His people: *"He found him in a desert land, and in the waste howling wilderness; he compassed him about, he cared for him, he kept him as the apple of his eye (ASV)."* The expression is literally "little man of the eye," like our little boy, pupil. The miniature of the person who looks into another's eye is reflected there. In Psalm 17:8 it is literally "little daughter of the eye." In the passage in Zechariah the word is literally "gate," the place where the rays of light pass to the retina. Why did God call Israel the apple of His eye?

This designation is a beautiful figure and picture of Israel because it speaks of, first, that which is so precious.

39

That Which Is So Precious

A man guards the apple of his eye because it is dear to him. It is considered by every man as one of his most precious possessions. The psalmist prayed to the Lord: *"Keep me as the apple of the eye; hide me in the shadow of Thy wings"* (Psalm 17:8). No one is interested in bargaining away the apple of his eye, nor in exchanging it for some trifling object. God considers the Jew as His precious possession. God has set His love on Israel and they are very precious to Him. Moses told them in the wilderness: *"'The* LORD *did not set His love on you nor choose you because you were more in number than any of the peoples, for you were the fewest of all peoples, but because the* LORD *loved you and kept the oath which He swore to your forefathers, the* LORD *brought you out by a mighty hand, and redeemed you from the house of slavery, from the hand of Pharaoh king of Egypt'"* (Deuteronomy 7:7-8).

G. H. Morrison once said: "There are books upon my shelves that I can never handle without a certain reverence and care, and I am gentle because they are of value to me. And the singular thing is that these precious volumes are not always the volumes that are the most finely bound. Some of them are little tattered creatures that a respectable servant longs to light the fire with.... So I take it God is gentle, because you and I are precious in His sight. He is infinitely patient with the worst of us because He values the worst of us so dearly." God loves Israel and they are precious to Him.

Second, the apple of the eye indicates that which is so easily injured.

That Which Is So Easily Injured

It is not necessary to thrust a knife into the eye to cause excruciating agony and injure it. A splinter, an eyelash, a speck of dust, or a touch will bring real pain. We need to be exceedingly careful how we conduct ourselves toward the Jew. He may appear without protector, but any injury hurts the heart of God, as He has repeatedly stated in the Word of God.

Third, the apple of the eye is that which is impossible to repair.

THAT WHICH IS IMPOSSIBLE TO REPAIR

Parts of the human body can be injured and mutilated, and yet some type of replacement can be made. Hands, feet, and bones in the body have been replaced by skillful surgeons, or so treated that they are still useful. There is a lot in the papers of the quadruple amputees and what is being done for their rehabilitation. But the pupil of the eye cannot be repaired once it is severely injured. Some injuries to Israel, God's people, cannot be repaired. How can the slaughter of six million Jews in Europe ever be repaired? How can this multiplied injury be righted? Impossible! And to think that every one who touched them—let alone cremated them—was touching the apple of God's eye!

Fourth, the apple of the eye is that which allows the light to penetrate.

THAT WHICH ALLOWS THE LIGHT TO PENETRATE

The pupil of the eye is the entrance through which the light rays from without penetrate to the retina so that we may see the objects before us. Israel is God's entrance way for the light of His Word and His salvation to enter the world. One day Jesus the Messiah said to a Samaritan woman: *"You worship that which you do not know; we worship that which we know; for salvation is from the Jews"* (John 4:22). These words of the Messiah and Saviour were in perfect accord with the declaration in Isaiah (43:10-12): *"'You are My witnesses,' declares the* LORD, *'and My servant whom I have chosen, in order that you may know and believe Me, and understand that I am He. Before Me there was no God formed, and there will be none after Me. I, even I, am the* LORD; *and there is no savior besides Me. It is I who have declared and saved and proclaimed, and there was no strange god among you; so you are My witnesses,' declares the* LORD, *'and I am God.'"* This was the intention of God for Israel and still is. It is sad that they are not letting the light shine to the peoples of the earth as God meant for them to do.

A Christian young man spent a summer in a lumber camp where he was surrounded by anything but Christian influences. Upon his return someone asked him, "Didn't you find it hard to live in such a place? Didn't the others jeer at you for being a Christian?"

"Oh," the young man said, "they never found out." Many in the world have never found out that Israel is God's gateway for His light to come into the world, and it is because Israel has been unwilling.

Fifth, the apple of the eye is that which is so carefully protected.

THAT WHICH IS SO CAREFULLY PROTECTED

Remarkable and abundant provision is made for the protection of the pupil of the eye, of which many people are unaware. The protection consists of: (1) the strong frontal bones (to guard against a blow); (2) the brow and eyelash (to protect against dust); (3) the lid (to guard against painful glare); and (4) the tear glands (to provide continuous cleansing). With Israel is the omnipotent power of God committed to protect them. The psalmist clearly recounts the protecting hand of God over His people: *"He has remembered His covenant forever, the word which He commanded to a thousand generations, the covenant which He made with Abraham, and His oath to Isaac. Then He confirmed it to Jacob for a statute, to Israel as an everlasting covenant, saying, 'To you I will give the land of Canaan, as the portion of your inheritance,' when they were only a few men in number, very few, and strangers in it. And they wandered about from nation to nation, from one kingdom to another people. He permitted* no man to oppress them, and He reproved kings for their sakes: 'Do not touch My anointed ones, and do My prophets no harm'" (Psalm 105:8-15). Remember, God's hand of protection is upon Israel as a nation, and He will not suffer them to cease as a people.

Jeremiah has one of the strongest affirmations of this truth in the Bible: *"Thus says the* LORD, *who gives the sun for light by day, and the fixed order of the moon and the stars for light by night, who stirs up the sea so that its waves roar; the* LORD *of hosts is His name: 'If this fixed order departs from before Me,' declares the* LORD, *'then the offspring of Israel also shall cease from being a nation before Me forever.' Thus says the* LORD, *'If the heavens above can be measured, and the foundations of the earth searched out below, then I will also cast off all the offspring of Israel for all that they have done,' declares the* LORD*"* (31:35-37). What could be more forceful than these words to assure us that God is determined to protect Israel, as a man zealously and carefully protects the very apple of his eye?

Last, the apple of the eye speaks of that which causes intense pain when injured.

THAT WHICH CAUSES INTENSE PAIN WHEN INJURED

When a man's pupil has been injured, he feels intense pain. And this pain can be so great that he becomes sick. To injure Israel is to cause God intense pain. He says: *"In all their affliction He was afflicted"* (Isaiah 63:9). When Israel is mistreated, God reckons that His very name, His own excellence, is blasphemed. (Isaiah 52:5).

We never dare to forget that he who touches Israel for ill, will not go unpunished. Nations as well as individuals have proved the truth of this passage of Scripture. On the other hand, we must also remember that he who touches Israel for good, will not go unrewarded (Matthew 25:40). You, too, have something you must keep in mind. You must be willing to open your eyes to see the glory and the beauty of the Messiah or you will never be able to behold the glorious sight.

A little boy was born blind. At last an operation was performed; the light was let in slowly. Then one day his mother led him out doors and uncovered his eyes, and for the first time in his life he saw the sky and the earth. "Mother!" he shouted. "Why did you not tell me it was so beautiful?"

She burst into tears as she said, "I tried to tell you, dear, but you could not understand me." So it is when we seek to tell Israel about the Messiah. Unless you open your eyes by the Spirit, you cannot understand. Open your eyes and see! If you are to give light to others, do not blind your own eyes!

Part 3

ISRAEL IN THE WRITINGS

5

The Similarities of
Job and Israel

FIRST STUDY: IN THE HANDS OF THE ENEMY

THIS BOOK is named after its chief character, Job, which means "persecuted" or "afflicted." In our canon it is the first of the poetic books of the Old Testament. Although the book is poetry, the story is not fiction but fact (cf. Ezekiel 14:14, 20; James 5:1). The events must have taken place in patriarchal times for (1) there is no mention of the Law; (2) the offerings are burnt offerings and not sin offerings as required under the Law; (3) Job performs the functions of a priest himself; and (4) no mention is made of the Exodus from Egypt. The book is a work unsurpassed for depth of feeling and grandeur of thought and conception. Luther said of it: "Magnificent and sublime as no other book of Scripture." Renan, the author and critic of the past century, said: "The Book of Job is the Hebrew book par excellence—it is in the Book of Job that the force, beauty, the depth of the Hebrew genius are seen at their best." Tennyson called it "the greatest poem of ancient or modern times." Carlyle said it was "apart from all theories about it, one of the greatest things ever written with pen. There is nothing written, I think, in the Bible or out of it, of equal merit."

The theme, subject, or problem of the book is the suffering of the godly. The suffering of the ungodly is no mystery. The psalmist said: *"Men of bloodshed and deceit will not live out*

47

half their days" (Psalm 55:23; cf. Proverbs 29:1). But why do
the godly suffer? The book really deals with five problems
that grow out of this main one and include it: (1) Can man
serve God disinterestedly from pure love of Him, or is all his
worship of God tainted with ulterior and selfish motives? (2)
Is there anyone but God to whom the control of the circumstances of human life can be attributed? (3) Are man's outward circumstances a criterion and standard of his moral
character and life before God? (4) Can men, by their wisdom,
rightly and completely comprehend the workings of the prov-
idence of God? (5) Since the righteous do endure such great
afflictions in this life, is a life of righteousness worth it in the
last analysis?

Scripture is so full in its truth that although there is but one
interpretation, there may be many applications. By way of
comparison with Job we can see the believer of this age exposed to himself by the dealings and chastenings of God,
judging himself, mistrusting himself, resting in the all-
sufficient grace of God. By way of contrast with Job we can
see Christ, the sinless Sufferer, doing God's will without murmuring and with complete trust in the wisdom and will of the
Father. By way of application we can discern in Job the
whole story of the salvation of the sinner.

An Englishman once said to Moody: "Did you ever notice
this, that the Book of Job is the key to the whole Bible? If
you understand Job you will understand the whole Bible!"

"No," said Moody, "I don't comprehend that. Job the key
to the whole Bible! How do you make that out?"

The Englishman said: "I divide Job into seven heads. The
first head is: A perfect man untried. That is what God said
about Job; that is Adam in Eden. He was perfect when God
put him there. The second head is: Tried by adversity. Job
fell, as Adam fell in Eden. The third head is: The wisdom of
the world. The world tried to restore Job; the three wise men
came to help him. That was the wisdom of the world centered
in those three men. You cannot," he said, "find any such eloquent language or wisdom anywhere, in any part of the

world, as those three men displayed, but they did not know anything about grace, and could not, therefore, help Job. Then in the fourth place comes the Daysman, that is Christ. In the fifth place, God speaks; and in the sixth, Job learns his lesson. 'I have heard of thee by the hearing of the ear: but now mine eye seeth thee. Wherefore I abhor myself, and repent in dust and ashes.' And then down came Job flat on the dunghill. The seventh head is this, that God restores him. Our last estate is better than our first."

By way of comparison, still further, Job is a picture of the nation Israel. This thought we carry through our three studies. For our purposes and true to the movement of the book we divide Job into three sections: chapters 1-3 speak of the suffering Job; chapters 4-31 set forth the sophistries of his friends; chapters 32-42 reveal the salvation or deliverance of Job by the Lord.

Job in His Suffering

First, let us note what kind of man Job was. Then let us consider his suffering, sorrow, and trial. This one delivered over into the hands of the enemy, Satan, was no ordinary man. He had wealth (cf. 1:3, 29:3, 6, 19). He knew the prosperity of the Lord. He was blessed with children (1:2) who are a heritage from the Lord. He was highly honored (29:7-11, 21-25). He was educated. He showed familiarity with writing, building, natural history, astronomy, and science in general. He was pious and godly (1:1, 5, 8; 2:3). He was perfect. This does not mean sinlessly perfect. He was perfect in the sense of complete as the word denotes (*tam*, from *tamam*, to be complete, whole). His godly life was well-rounded, not zealous in some things and lax in others. He was as honest in public as in private; he was as true with men as with God. He was upright, sincere, and straightforward, as we say "on the level." He feared God. God was the center of his life and desire. He lived in the presence of God. He turned away from evil, shunning every form of it. He was concerned for the spiritual well-being of his children (1:5); this was not spasmodic but a constant practice of his. This is brought out by two features of the original text: first, the words, "all the days," and second, the verb in the imperfect denotes that which is continuous and reiterated. He always concerned himself for the needy (29:12-17).

Just as Job was an extraordinary man, so was his trial unusual at the hand of the enemy, Satan. Job was tried in his circumstances, or circumstantially; in his body, or physically; and in his faith, or spiritually. He lost all his wealth and property. He lost his children, dearer far than his riches. And all of this transpired with satanic speed and suddenness. He lost his health.

Someone has described it: "The disease of Job seems to have been a universal ulcer, producing an eruption over his entire person, and attended with violent pain and constant restlessness. A universal boil, or group of boils, over the body would accord with the account of the disease in the various parts of the book. In elephantiasis the skin is covered with incrustations like those of an elephant. It is a chronic and contagious disease, marked by a thickening of the legs, with a loss of hair and feeling, a swelling of the face, and a hoarse, nasal voice. It affects the whole body: the bones as well as the skin are covered with spots, and tumors, at first red, but afterwards black."

Payson was asked, when under great bodily affliction, whether he could see any particular reason for such dealings of God with him. "No," he said, "but I am as well satisfied as if I could see ten thousand; God's will is the very perfection of all reason." So reasoned Job in his trial. Then Job lost the help and sympathetic understanding of his wife. Through all these tests Job stood firm and glorified God.

Israel in Her Suffering
What a parallel to these things does the nation Israel afford! She too was highly favored of God. God delighted in

her. He called her the apple of His eye, His chosen, His son. He even called her His Jeshurun (the same root word as "upright" used of Job), His upright one (Deuteronomy 32:15, 33:26; Isaiah 44:2). She too was prosperous under the hand of God (Deuteronomy 8:18). God gave her power to acquire wealth. Just as Satan resisted God's word of commendation and joy in Job, so has he done and still does with regard to Israel (Zechariah 3:1 ff.).

God delivered Job permissively into the hands and devices of the enemy Satan for dreadful trials. In a similar manner God delivered over the dearly beloved of His soul into the hands of her enemies (Jeremiah 12:7). As Job was stripped of all, so was Israel (Lamentations 5:1-5). This is true in a greater measure today than it was in Jeremiah's day when he wrote the Lamentations. Many were the waves and billows of woe that came over Job. How many and of what magnitude have they been that have swept over Israel and still engulf her in this hour!

First, she was persecuted of Pharaoh upon arriving at nationhood. Then the nations on the wilderness journey, especially Amalek, vented their wrath on her. In later years Haman took up the cudgel of persecution against her to exterminate her. Antiochus Epiphanes in the second century before Christ joined himself to the number of those who can be called the inveterate and unrelenting enemies of Israel.

The Middle Ages saw wave after wave of destruction break over the defenseless head of the nation of the weary foot and the weary heart. If thousands died in plagues from contaminated waters, it was Israel who had committed the dastardly deed, although many of her own number perished. If a Gentile child were found dead near the time of Passover, it was the community of God's people that had perpetrated the crime in order to have the blood for ritual purposes, although it was known that Israel turned with loathing from all blood in their ritual and in their food according to the explicit prohibitions of the Mosaic Law. The long, sad, bloodstained story of the Spanish Inquisition has never been fully told, and it is best to pass it over in some degree of silence. And what shall we say of her present-day privations, wanderings, and sorrows? And the end is definitely not yet. Israel's history has been a long concatenation of woes.

But we must realize what Job's friends had to learn: that not all suffering is retributive. God's greatest trials are inflicted upon the strongest, for by His grace they are enpowered to bear them. If Job had only known what God had said to Satan and how His heart went out to Job in his trial! If Israel only knew what God has said of her in His Word to Satan and all men and how His heart yearns for her! Here we have exemplified clearly the truth that whom the Lord loveth He chasteneth. Satan in the last analysis strikes at God by implying that He can only be loved with a mercenary love and only for His benefits do human creatures feel drawn to Him. When the human heart really catches a glimpse of the love in the heart of God, it responds with love. *"We love him, because he first loved us"* (1 John 4:19, KJV).

Spurgeon, while visiting a friend's home in the country, was attracted to a beautiful weather vane which the friend had placed upon the cupola of a new barn. On the weather vane were inscribed the words, "God is love." Spurgeon expressed surprise at the choice of such a motto for such a place and said, "What do you mean by putting that text of Scripture on the weather vane? Do you mean that God's love is as changeable as the wind?"

"Oh, no," said the friend, "I mean to say that God is love whichever way the wind blows."

Job learned this truth; Israel as a nation will yet learn it. No matter what the trial, how deep the sorrow, how cutting the wound, how painful the disease, how loathesome the affliction, how unbearable the circumstances, God is always and ever love. And He chastens those whom He loves.

In these first chapters we have seen that God permits the godly to suffer for the glory of God. In the remainder of the poem it is seen that the godly suffer for their own good as well.

What is as evident as the afflictions imposed by Satan upon Job is the protection afforded him by God. Satan in his venom could go only thus far and no farther. Throughout the centuries Satan has longed to blot out Israel, but she knows God's protecting hand. It is said of Felix of Nola that when he was hotly pursued by murderers, he took refuge in a cave, and instantly over the rift of it the spiders wove their webs. Seeing the web, the murderers passed by. Then said this saint. "Where God is not, a wall is but a spider's web; where God is, a spider's web is as a wall." How true for Job and how true for Israel!

SECOND STUDY: AT THE MERCY OF THE CRITICS

Most of the Book of Job is taken up with the addresses of Job's friends and his answers to them. They are not incidental to the book but are of primary importance. To view them otherwise is to lose sight of the great movement of the book. These friends attempt as best they can to probe Job's predicament. He does not understand the reason for his unusual sufferings, nor do they. It is no small problem with which these men are wrestling. There is no book in the Bible that does not have some reference to trial. The book of Psalms has 150 psalms and over 90 have some reference to suffering. There is no believer in the Scriptures whose history we have in any fullness at all, who was not called upon to endure trouble and suffering in some form. Many times the most godly were the most tried. Review for a moment the lives of such men as Abraham, Isaac, Jacob, Joseph, Moses, David, Daniel, Paul, Peter, the early disciples and apostles. Did not each one find out experientially the truth of the words: *"'For man is born for trouble, as sparks fly upward'"* (Job 5:7)? Those who were greatly used of God were trained in the school of affliction and hardship.

Job Under the Critic's Scrutiny

Job's friends, in trying to explain his afflictions, really misrepresented God as well as Job, and so were Satan's tool to cause Job to renounce God. Job's heart felt it could not accept their opinions as God's dealings with him. These friends were prominent, wise, and pious men of age and experience. Their arguments were good and forceful, but they were based on wrong premises. Job refused to admit the cogency of their arguments because he knew of his own innocence of their charges against him. The arguments of Job's friends went from veiled insinuations to open denunciations. As the argument progressed the friends realized that they were unable to convince him, and they became more and more harsh and severe.They began mildly but were astonished that Job tried to refute some of their primary arguments, and finally they lost confidence in his uprightness and sincerity. Instead of applying a balm, wine, and oil to his wounds, they cauterized them, pouring in vitriol. It is always like vinegar on soda for someone to come to a broken soul and dejected spirit prattling about platitudes without sympathy.

The main contention of Job's friends was that suffering is for sin. This is true in general but far from true in all cases. As a matter of fact, Job's sufferings were not the result of sin so much as they were the trial of his righteousness, the trial of his faith. His friends reasoned that something grievous must have been the matter with Job; and because they could not see it, they concluded he was a hypocrite hiding his sin and his real self. Job's friends made him writhe more than Satan had. They did him more harm than the devil. When Job knew his friends were wrong in their contentions, he was stirred to resentment against them. Throughout the words of the friends there is special pleading; they did not state the whole case at all. His friends were merely speaking truths they had learned from memory; he spoke his words from a tortured and anguished and agonized heart. Though his comforters, miserable as they were, pelted him with inconsiderate words, he had more faith than any one of them (Job 13:15).

Note the trend of reasoning of each adviser. Eliphaz the Temanite held that all men are sinners, and sin is connected with suffering. He did not at first doubt the sincerity of Job nor his integrity. He said: *"'Remember now, who ever perished being innocent? Or where were the upright destroyed?'"* (4:7). His principle was true in general but does not explain special suffering. What of the case of Abel? Was he not upright and righteous and did he not perish, being destroyed by the hand of his murderous brother?

The other friends seemed to get their point of departure from Eliphaz, and followed his reasoning, but more and more cast doubts on the piety of Job. He appealed again and again to his own observation and experience. Notice "according to what I have seen" in 4:8 and "I have seen" in 5:3 as well as the recital of his vision in his dream recorded in 4:12-21 (see also 15:17). When he spoke in his second address he charged Job with guilt. He set forth his indictment thus: *"'Indeed, you do away with reverence, and hinder meditation before God. For your guilt teaches your mouth, and you choose the language of the crafty. Your own mouth condemns you, and not I; and your own lips testify against you'"* (15:4-6).

In his third and last address he administered a scathing rebuke to Job, accusing him of downright wickedness. Hear the severity of his words: *"'Is not your wickedness great, and your iniquities without end?'"* (22:5). He went on to charge Job with stripping the naked of their clothing, with withholding water from the weary and bread from the hungry, with turning away widows with emptiness, and with robbing the fatherless of their maintenance and stay. Think of it. Contrast this, if you will, with the statement God made concerning Job at the outset of the book and with Job's own recital of his former days in 29:11-13; 31:16-23. Carrying Eliphaz's argument to its logical conclusion, we would find that the most sinful men were the most afflicted.

Bildad the Shuhite appealed to tradition. He ordered his argument after this manner: *"'Please inquire of past genera-*

tions, and consider the things searched out by their fathers. For we are only of yesterday and know nothing, because our days on earth are as a shadow. Will they not teach you and tell you, and bring forth words from their minds?'" (8:8-10). Tradition is just the observation of a number of men, and many times is no more correct than individual observation. He should have appealed to an objective norm and standard, God's own revelation to man, in that measure in which God had already made Himself known in that day. In his second address Bildad prefaced his words with the statement: *"'Indeed, the light of the wicked goes out, and the flame of his fire gives no light'"* (18:5), and then went on to enumerate the multiplied calamities and adversities that assuredly befall the wicked. His last answer to Job was quite brief, and he contented himself with admonishing Job that man can by no means be pure and just before God when even the stars are not pure in His sight (chapters 18, 25).

Zophar the Naamathite was the third friend, and he felt he must speak forth his word of consolation and comfort also. He appealed to the law principle (not the Law of Moses, for it was not yet given). He stated his position thus: *"'Know then that God forgets a part of your iniquity'"* (11:6b). If God were an exacting God, where would sinful man be? The psalmist asks this same question: *"If Thou, Lord, shouldst mark iniquities, O Lord, who could stand?"* (Psalm 130:3). In his second and last address Zophar pointed out that the triumphing of the wicked is short and that he perishes forever like his own dung (20:5-7). He closed summarily with the words: *"'This is the wicked man's portion from God, even the heritage decreed to him by God'"* (20:29). Zophar was quite severe and denunciatory in his charges, as one would expect of a legalist. Boiling down the words of a legalist to the basic residuum, we shall always find him saying, "It's good for you that you are in such a plight. You are getting just what you deserve and even less. You have no cause to complain."

All these men based God's infliction of suffering, or permission of it, on a basis of justice (for sin) rather than on a basis of love. They were miserable comforters (16:2) and physicians of no value (13:4); they gave the impression that they were the people, and wisdom would die with them (12:2). How like so many critics of our day were these critics! Their criticisms too often were the opposite of the truth. Satan's afflictions were sore, but the criticisms of Job's friends were far worse.

Israel Under the Critics' Scrutiny

Since Israel has been suffering for centuries she has not lacked for critics, self-appointed, self-sustained, and assuredly self-opinionated, to tell her the reason for her trials. Zechariah gives a timely word here. In chapter 1 of his prophecy, after noting the lessons for post-captivity Israel in the history of their forefathers' disobedience and punishment, he declares God's love and jealousy for Israel. God says through the prophet: *"'But I am very angry with the nations who are at ease; for while I was only a little angry, they furthered the disaster'"* (1:15). It is as though a father were reluctantly punishing his own child with a stick or with a word of rebuke or restraint, and a stranger came to chasten with a rod of iron. God scattered Israel (Jeremiah 31:10), but the nations made her howl (Isaiah 52:5).

Isaiah tells Babylon: *"'I was angry with My people, I profaned My heritage, and gave them into your hand. You did not show mercy to them, on the aged you made your yoke very heavy,'"* (47:6). The contrast that the prophet draws between God's treatment of Israel and the dealings of the nations with the chosen people is marked. The critics of Israel ask: "Have not the trials of the Jews been minutely predicted by Moses and the prophets?" This question goes on the false assumption that God sanctions all that He predicts. By the same token God would have to approve of all wars, for Christ said there would be wars and rumors of wars. Also, the sufferings of Christ were foretold in detail, but still the Holy Spirit notes that it was with "wicked hands" (implying responsibility) He was crucified and slain.

Some say: "It is too bad the poor Jews have to suffer, but they have it coming to them." On the same ground, which one of us, apart from grace, does not have infinitely more "coming to us"? Then, again, what of the saved Jews in the present suffering in Europe? (We understand that saved Gentiles form the Body of Christ; but to the persecuting unsaved world, all Jews are alike.) Will not the remnant of the Tribulation time suffer though they be righteous? (Cf. the imprecatory psalms.) Would the critics say that these godly ones have it coming to them also? Many are satisfied in thinking that the Jews are suffering because they have objectionable traits, personal and otherwise. Is not this the same method that Job's friends used? Because these critics do not understand the real reason, they feel they must find any petty reason to offer as the cause for Israel's trials.

Those who blame the Jews' sufferings on the crucifixion of Christ feel they have solved the problem satisfactorily. Obviously no words of man can in the least mitigate the guilt attached to Israel for the rejection of Christ as noted in the gospel narratives. But are there not features worth noting in this regard? Do not the words of Christ, "Father, forgive them; for they know not what they do" have some bearing on the question? The list of culprits in Acts 4:27 is also illuminating. Still others say that the very plight of Israel proves that they are so sinful God never chose them as His people. If God did not choose them when He said the words of Isaiah 44:1-2, then He never chose any believer today when He says, *"He chose us in Him before the foundation of the world"* (Ephesians 1:4).

We are aware that the choice of Israel is national to earthly privilege and that of the believer is individual to heavenly privilege, but we are speaking now only of the surety and certainty of the divine, sovereign choice. How unfair and cruel and inhumane and unfeeling and harsh, yes, almost savage and barbarous, have been many of the criticisms against Israel. She knows full well how Job felt when pelted with unfeeling words from self-styled physicians.

St. Augustine related the story of the man who complained to Almighty God about a neighbor, saying, "O Lord, take away this wicked person." And God said, "Which?" How foolhardy to judge without the mind of God. He shall bring to light the hidden things, so we can afford to refrain from the act of judging the suffering and the tried. May God grant that we shall not be found in the role of critic or judge of His suffering people Israel.

THIRD STUDY: FACE TO FACE WITH THE LORD

The book of Job reveals a victory, but it is not the victory of man's remarkable reasoning nor the victory of superior argumentation, but the blessed victory of faith (13:15). This triumph was not won in a moment nor by one leap, but in definite and progressive stages. When the last words of Job are given in chapter 31, his friends were still of the same opinion and Job still held his conviction. The problem was deadlocked, as it were. The argument of the book is summarized in 32:1-3: *"Then these three men ceased answering Job, because he was righteous in his own eyes. But the anger of Elihu the son of Barachel the Buzite, of the family of Ram burned; against Job his anger burned, because he justified himself before God. And his anger burned against his three friends because they had found no answer, and yet had condemned Job."*

Then Elihu comes preparing the way for the words of the Lord which follow.We take his words as appropriate because the Lord utters no rebuke of him later. In a sense he is the answer to Job's burning desire that he might have a Daysman (*mochiah*, lit., an umpire, arbiter) to stand between God and himself (9:33).

The burden of Elihu's several addresses is: (1) God is infinitely and eternally greater than man in power. In view of this it behooves man to be in a place of submission before his Creator. (2) God is infinitely greater than man in wisdom. He has no need to detail His ways and plans to man, even if man could understand them (33:13). Man does best when he awaits God's solution which He alone can give and will give when it pleases Him. (3) God is infinitely greater than man in righteousness. *"Far be it from God to do wickedness, and from the Almighty to do wrong. Surely, God will not act wickedly, and the Almighty will not pervert justice'"* (34:10, 12). It is impossible for us fully to conceive how sinful it is for us to condemn the righteous and just God, or seek to maintain our righteousness at the expense of His. (4) God is infinitely greater than man in His tender mercy (James 5:11). If we could understand the heart of God, we would be convinced that even in our afflictions which He permits, His heart is most tender and compassionate toward us. After these addresses, God Himself appears. But He is not on the defensive, for He is responsible and amenable to none of His creatures.

Job in the Presence of God

Neither the enemy nor the critics dealt properly with Job and his problem: that remained for God alone to do. Job had been afflicted inwardly and outwardly; now God intended to bless him inwardly and outwardly. God did this by asking Job nearly a hundred questions. (If one is ever inclined to feel quite exalted in his own mind, we suggest that he read through these questions. It is a most beneficial and deflating experience.) Suffice it to say, that Job failed in all his examination questions. But the result was blessed, nevertheless. God revealed to Job the omnipotence and omniscience which are God's alone. Nowhere in the Bible is there a more marvelous delineation of the majesty and greatness of God. This revealed to Job his own ignorance (and of earthly, temporal things at that). Then God set forth the impotence of Job. This was not done to show Job that His ways were totally inscrutable. If so, then why appear at all in this problem if not to solve it Himself? No, the portrayal of the frailty and weakness of Job was meant to give him a clearer conception of the glorious nature of his Creator.

Job's arguments showed that he had an imperfect, or rather an incomplete, view of God. The pivot and climax of the book are verses 5 and 6 of chapter 42. Job says: *"'I have heard of Thee by the hearing of the ear; but now my eye sees Thee; therefore I retract, and I repent in dust and ashes.'"* This is the height of the piety and faith of the afflicted one when brought to repentance. Job's righteousness was real, for God had boasted of it to Satan. But in the light of God it appeared as nothing. Such is the repentance of the righteous. He might try to clear himself before men; before God this was impossible. The vision of God had turned hearsay into clear vision. Hearsay is that which is taught us, what we receive by tradition or instruction, what might be termed the letter of the truth. (We dare not press this out of bounds, for Job did utter words of faith and truth in chapters 13 and 19).

Vision, on the other hand, is that view which is unclouded, undimmed, untrammeled sight, having the eye filled to overflowing with the knowledge of God. That Job did not know God in all the perfection of His Being is clear from the view of God that he then expressed. It is direct and soul-searching experiences together with the realization of God's power, majesty, holiness, love, and goodness that turn hearsay into vision. He saw clearly then that what he had mistaken for the seizure of an enemy was the firm grasp of a friend, and what he thought was the weapon of a foe was the careful and skillful physician who only cuts to heal. The skillful physician may hurt, but he does not injure. Is this not true of our God?

By God's appearing to him, Job learned himself. Once having seen God, he saw himself. He saw himself in all his impurity. When the seraphim stand before God they veil their faces before His holiness. When Isaiah saw the Lord he saw his own unclean lips and said, "Woe is me!" When Paul saw Christ he fell to the ground as dead. When Peter saw Christ he said, "Depart from me; for I am a sinful man, O Lord." When John saw the Lord he said, "I fell at his feet as dead." In God's sight all our comeliness is turned into corruption; in

His purity and whiteness all on earth is polluted and blackness of darkness.

To see God as infinite is to see ourselves as finite. To see Him as perfect is to bring us forcibly to our imperfection. To know Him as all-knowing, the summation of all wisdom, is to realize our ignorance. To acknowledge Him as right is to admit ourselves as wrong. To view His holiness is to be smitten with our own sin and contamination. Submission, contribution, and humility should then follow. Job, then, came forth with a clearer vision of God, a discrediting of self, a rejecting of self-righteousness.

When the spiritual and the inward had been cared for, then God showered upon the patriarch the temporal and the outward. He became the channel of blessing through his intercession for his friends who had so grievously maligned him. Such intercession surely was a humiliating thing for them. *"And the* LORD *restored the fortunes of Job when he prayed for his friends, and the* LORD *increased all that Job had twofold"* (42:10). Job's enemy dealt ill with him; his friends dealt with him as best they could; it is God who ever and always deals best with us. How true, then, the words of the apostle James, *"You have heard of the endurance of Job and have seen the outcome* [the final experience that came into the life of Job by the Lord's command and direction] *of the Lord's dealings, that the Lord is full of compassion and is merciful"* (James 5:11).

Israel in the Presence of God

The blessedness which was the portion of Job in the presence of God, meeting Him face to face, will be the experience of Israel in a coming day. Zechariah predicts: *"'And I will pour out on the house of David and on the inhabitants of Jerusalem, the Spirit of grace and of supplication, so that they will look on Me whom they have pierced; and they will mourn for Him... like the bitter weeping over a first-born'"* (12:10). In that selfsame time *"'a fountain will be opened for the house of David and for the inhabitants of Jerusalem, for sin and for impurity'"* (13:1). Job, looking unto God, saw his own undone condition and was cleansed; Israel will see the returning "Hope of Israel" and will be fully cleansed.

Then shall come to pass the words of Jeremiah: *"'In those days and at that time,' declares the Lord, 'search will be made for the iniquity of Israel, but there will be none; and for the sins of Judah, but they will not be found; for I shall pardon those whom I leave as a remnant'"* (50:20). How glorious will be the lot of God's ancient people when Israel is without iniquity and Judah without sins! By the appearing of the Lord to Job, he came to know God as never before; when God appears to Israel, they shall know Him as never before. God's law will be implanted in their hearts in such a fashion that they will not need to teach their neighbor in the knowledge of the Lord, for they shall all know Him from the least of them to the greatest (Jeremiah 31:31-34).

By coming face to face with the Lord they will finally understand and know themselves. They will repent in deep sorrow, mourning, and contrition. They will throw to the bats and to the moles all their vaunted self-righteousness. As with Job, their former knowledge of God will appear shallow in comparison with the light of that hour. Job was seeking after God and found Him; so will Israel.

The hour of Job's deliverance was one of most intense pain, and mental and spiritual anxiety. Such will be the case with Israel. Regathered and settled in the land, the eyes of the confederacies of the Gentile nations will be attracted to her. The confederacy in the north of Europe, that in the south of Europe (the revived Roman Empire with its ten kingdoms), that of the kings of the sun-rising, and the king of the north of Palestine will sweep down upon the defenseless land with rapacity and avarice, to make of her a spoil. Zechariah foretold that all the nations would be gathered together against the holy city of Jerusalem to make war with her. Israel has had many a dark hour in her national history; this will be the worst of all and the culmination of them all. She

will have her time of trouble and trial, but God's Word is sure
that she will be saved out of it (Jeremiah 30:7).

Israel will then, as Job, know increased prosperity as never
before. *"Jerusalem will be inhabited without walls, because
of the multitude of men and cattle within it. Grain will make
the young men flourish, and new wine the virgins'"* (Zechariah 2:4; 9:17*b*). That will be the time when Israel will become
a channel of blessing to others. First Job was blessed, then his
friends through him. The order is the same with Israel and the
Gentiles. As Psalm 67 puts it: when the LORD blesses Israel, it
will follow that all the ends of the earth will fear Him. Israel
will enter actually into the fulfillment of God's original purpose for her: a kingdom of priests and a holy nation (Exodus
19:5-6). Ten men out of all the languages of the nations shall
lay hold of the Jew and desire to go with him, recognizing
that God is with him. Job is a wonderful character; Israel is a
remarkable people; but how blessed is God above all! He is
ready to forgive and pardon and receive. This God is our
blessed, daily portion.

The problem of Job is solved; that of Israel will be too.
Then it will be seen that afflictions try piety as well as
iniquity. Trials develop faith. Hardships lead to clearer views
of God. Tribulations draw the soul nearer to God. What was
formerly considered an unbearable burden is seen to be an
abiding blessing. What matters then if God permits us to be
delivered into the hands of the enemy, or allows us to be sub-
jected to the vitriolic ministrations of physicians of no value,
as long as at the end of it all we may have that meeting with
Him face to face, to minister to our every need? Thrice
blessed be God for Himself and for His all-sufficient
provisions!

6

Israel's Exaltation Above
All Nations

THE PROMISE OF GOD is that Israel would be the head of the
nations when living in obedience to the Lord. Through Moses
the word had been given that *"'The* LORD *shall make you the
head and not the tail, and you only shall be above, and you
shall not be underneath, if you will listen to the commandments of the* LORD *your God, which I charge you today, to
observe them carefully, and do not turn aside from any of the
words which I command you today, to the right or to the left,
to go after other gods to serve them'"* (Deuteronomy
28:13-14). Many centuries later the same Spirit spoke through
the prophet Zechariah: *"Thus says the* LORD *of hosts, 'In
those days ten men from the nations of every language will
grasp the garment of a Jew saying, "Let us go with you, for
we have heard that God is with you"'"* (Zechariah 8:23). But
through the past many centuries Israel has been the tail of the
nations rather than the head. Will she ever be in that place of
prominence and eminence which God has foretold for her?
The answer is sure and is found in Psalm 45.

The psalm is a marriage song celebrating the marriage of
the king. Some have referred it to the marriage of Solomon to
the daughter of Pharaoh of Egypt. A number of other views
have been proposed seeking to identify the passage with one
king or another, but none can be considered weightier than
that which applies it to Solomon. Yet Solomon himself does
not entirely meet all the requirements of the passage. A

greater than Solomon is spoken of here, and so we find a skillful blending of the human and the divine. The Messianic interpretation is the most ancient among both Jews and Christians. The Chaldee paraphrase on verse 2 reads, "Thy beauty, O King Messiah, is greater than that of the sons of men." The selection gives the union of the Messiah with His Bride under the figure of a marriage feast.

The psalm has a simple threefold division: (1) the praise of the King's beauty and majesty (vv. 1-9); (2) the praise of the queen (vv. 10-15); (3) the promise of the King's perpetuity (vv. 16-17).

THE PRAISE OF THE KING'S BEAUTY AND MAJESTY
(PSALM 45:1-9)

The title of the psalm, all too often overlooked in consideration of passages in the Psalter, reveals (1) that it is set to *Shoshannim* (that is, lilies); (2) it is from the sons of Korah; (3) it is a *Maskil* (instruction) psalm; and (4) it is a song of loves. Lilies are a splendid type of the Lord Jesus Christ in His purity and beauty. The song of loves describes the relation of the Messiah in His love toward His Bride, then toward Israel, and all of the nations upon the earth.

The title thus prepares us for the content of the psalm by striking the keynote. The sons of Korah, writing in the singular person, speak first of the reaction of the truth they are to impart upon their own hearts. *"My heart overflows with a good theme;"* reads the psalm, *"I address my verses to the King; my tongue is the pen of a ready writer"* (Psalm 45:1). It is unusual in Hebrew poetry for the writer to tell of the greatness of his subject and how full his heart is of it. The word "overflows" is literally "boils up," the figure either from boiling water or from a bubbling fountain.

The work of the writer is for the King, that is, dedicated to the King Messiah. The King is now described: *"Thou art fairer than the sons of men; grace is poured upon Thy lips; therefore God has blessed Thee forever"* (Psalm 45:2). The beauty and eloquence of the King are first extolled. The word "fairer" is the Hebrew word for beautiful reduplicated, the only time this occurs in the Old Testament. So greatly would the Spirit of God emphasize this thought, that He has coined a word. The King is fair beyond all human standard or comparison. This is His moral beauty and glory primarily. Therefore, seeing there is such beauty in Him, there is but one conclusion: that God has blessed Him forever.

In the next three verses are the mighty conquests of the King when He comes as Judge, girded with a sword and ready for battle (Revelation 19:11-21). The Messiah is addressed: *"Gird Thy sword on Thy thigh, O Mighty One, in Thy splendor and Thy majesty! And in Thy majesty ride on victoriously, for the cause of truth and meekness and righteousness; let Thy right hand teach Thee awesome things. Thy arrows are sharp; the peoples fall under Thee; Thy arrows are in the heart of the King's enemies"* (Psalm 45:3-5). This is the second coming when the Lord Jesus will appear to judge the world in righteousness. He will then be in conflict with the enemies of His beleaguered people, Israel. He will avenge and save the remnant of His people.

See Psalm 110 and Zechariah 12 and 14. He prospers in His campaign to vindicate truth, righteousness, and meekness as against fraud, sin, and haughtiness. His victory will be complete, for His arrows will be in the heart of His enemies, an emphatic way of stating their complete subjugation. Because the victory has been accomplished, the Messianic throne, long since promised, will be set up. *"Thy throne, O God, is forever and ever; a scepter of uprightness is the scepter of Thy kingdom"* (Psalm 45:6). It is noteworthy that the Messiah is directly addressed, not by symbol or type or figure, as God; proof positive is given in Hebrews 1. The throne to be set up at the defeat of the enemies is the promised throne of the Davidic Covenant (2 Samuel 7:13, 16; Psalm 89).

But what qualifications does the King have for rulership? Some men are excellent on the battlefield but are not fitted for government. But the Messiah has all necessary requirements. It is said of him: *"Thou hast loved righteousness, and hated wickedness; therefore God, Thy God, has anointed Thee with the oil of joy above Thy fellows"* (Psalm 45:7). The moral qualities of the King are superb: He is a great lover and a great hater. He loves righteousness, not merely has an admiration for it; He hates wickedness, not merely has a dislike for it. Such being His credentials, He was to be a supremely happy King.

When we read Isaiah 53:3 concerning the Man of Sorrows, we must remember also that He prayed His joy might be fulfilled in His disciples (John 17:13). Some interpret the "fellows" of verse 7 to mean other kings, but it is better to define it as the Church revealed in the New Testament. Here the Church is spoken of by figure. The Church appears in the Old Testament only by way of type, figure, or illustration; it is not there present in manifestation or in prophecy. The climax is the marriage feast and this is given in full Oriental setting: *"All Thy garments are fragrant with myrrh and aloes and cassia; out of ivory palaces stringed instruments have made Thee glad. Kings' daughters are among Thy noble ladies; at Thy right hand stands the queen in gold from Ophir"* (Psalm 45:8-9).

The marriage feast prophesied of in Revelation 19:7 is pictured here. Thank God for the joy and gladness that shall be His in that day. The kings' daughters in the retinue of the queen are the representatives of the nations in the kingdom. The queen herself is the Church, the Bride of the Messiah, by way of figure. In the Old Testament Israel is seen as the wife of the Lord, and never as the Bride of the Messiah. This position belongs to the redeemed of this age. She is arrayed in wondrous beauty and righteousness, but the King is deservedly the center of attraction. In the blessed Word it is Christ all and in all. Luther was indeed right: there is but one Book and in it all is written of Him.

The Praise of the Queen (Psalm 45:10-15)

The queen is now addressed in the following words: *"Listen, O daughter, give attention and incline your ear; forget your people and your father's house; then the King will desire your beauty; because He is your Lord, bow down to Him"* (Psalm 45:10-11). The queen is counseled to adapt herself to her new relationships. She is to forget her past and devote herself to the King, so that His affection may be completely centered upon her. And not only that, but she shall receive honor on every hand. *"And the daughter of Tyre will come with a gift; the rich among the people will entreat your favor"* (Psalm 45:12). All the nations will seek the favor of the queen ("your favor" is feminine in the Hebrew).

The marriage procession is next depicted. *"The King's daughter is all glorious within; her clothing is interwoven with gold. She will be led to the King in embroidered work; the virgins, her companions who follow her, will be brought to Thee. They will be led forth with gladness and rejoicing; they will enter into the King's palace"* (Psalm 45:13-15). The queen in Oriental fashion is waiting in her Father's house to be escorted to her bridegroom's home. It will be first the rapture and then the marriage. She is led to her Beloved's home with her attendants and walks in, in Oriental fashion, on richly woven carpets, with attendants and music. The virgins, her companions in the place of nearest intimacy to the Bride, are the remnant of Israel. (Cf. Matthew 25:1-13.) Israel will then be the head of the nations to go into the millennial reign. This will be the hour of Israel's exaltation.

The Promise of the King's Perpetuity (Psalm 45:16-17)

The King is now the recipient of the best wish the Orientalist can conceive of: the joy of a progeny. *"In place of Thy fathers will be Thy sons; Thou shalt make them princes in all the earth"* (Psalm 45:16). In the place of ancestors there will be the descendants of the Messiah. The sons of the Messiah are His spiritual seed. Isaiah tells us that when the Messiah has prolonged His days (a reference to the resurrection of Christ), He shall see His seed (Isaiah 53:10; Psalm 22:30-31). In the Orient today, Christians are called the family of the Messiah. The writer speaks as one in a long line of inspired heralds of the Messiah, when he concludes: *"I will cause Thy name to be remembered in all generations; therefore the peoples will give Thee thanks forever and ever"* (Psalm 45:17). The picture of the King is glorious, but such also is that of the queen (the Church) and her virgins (Israel) who will occupy a place of eminence in the Kingdom of the Messiah.

God has great things in His Book and in His heart for Israel. May we be thinking God's thoughts after Him.

7

Israel and the World's Conversion

PSALM 67 is one of the shorter psalms in the Bible, but it is one of great significance for Israel and her spiritual position in the world. It reads thus: *"For the choir director; with stringed instruments. A Psalm. A Song. God be gracious to us and bless us, and cause His face to shine upon us (Selah). That Thy way may be known on the earth, Thy salvation among all nations. Let the peoples praise Thee, O God; let all the peoples praise Thee. Let the nations be glad and sing for joy; for Thou wilt judge the peoples with uprightness, and guide the nations on the earth (Selah). Let the peoples praise Thee, O God; let all the peoples praise Thee. The earth has yielded its produce; God, our God, blesses us. God blesses us, that all the ends of the earth may fear Him"* (Psalm 67).

Along with Psalms 65 and 66, this one forms a trilogy. The psalm is usually understood as a psalm of thanksgiving for the blessings and joys of the harvest. These picture the blessings which Israel and the nations will enjoy in the days of the reign of the Messiah. Though the psalm be small in scope, yet it contains within it the secret of all missions and the unchangeable order of God for world blessing and conversion.

The psalmist speaks, first of all, of God's blessing and its result.

God's Blessing and Its Result (Psalm 67:1-2)

The psalm begins with a threefold petition. The prayer is that God will bless His ancient people Israel, that He will be merciful to them, and that He will cause His face to shine upon them. God's pardon and forgiveness are basic to all His dealings with His creatures. Israel must first experience and know the mercy of God in the pardon of sin, and this only through the Messiah and His work. How God's great mercy pursues every sinner!

A professional diver said he had in his house what would probably strike a visitor as a very strange ornament: the shells of an oyster holding fast a piece of printed paper. He was diving on the coast when he observed this oyster on a rock at the bottom of the sea with a piece of paper in its mouth. He detached it and began to read through the goggles of his headpiece. It was a Gospel tract, and coming to him thus strangely and unexpectedly, it so impressed his unconverted heart that he said, "I can hold out against God's mercy in Christ no longer, since it pursues me thus." He became, while in the ocean's depth, a repentant, converted, and sin-forgiven man. He was saved at the bottom of the sea. The mercy of God reaches to the lowest depths.

The second part of the petition is that God will bless His people. The thought of blessing is prominent here, as in verses 6 and 7 also. The threefold priestly blessing of Numbers 6:24-26 is in mind. Aaron was charged to bless God's people, saying, *"The* Lord *bless you, and keep you; the* Lord *make His face shine on you, and be gracious to you; the* Lord *lift up His countenance on you, and give you peace.'"* The shining of God's face upon them is manifestation of His favor and pleasure. This is to be realized not only upon them, but literally with them, in the sense of accompanying them on their way.

God's presence is to be with them to lighten, to cheer, and to bless. The shout of the King shall yet be in the midst of Israel. Verses 1 to 3 show that to experience the mercy of God is to know Him and to know Him is to praise Him. The psalmist makes it clear that the prayer for blessing and mercy is not a selfish one to stop with the recipient. It is asked for in order that God's gracious dealings and providences, that is, His way, may be known throughout the length and breadth of the earth, and that His saving grace may be experienced among all nations.

This is blessed fulfillment of the promise to Abraham that through his seed all the families of the earth would be blessed. Psalm 98:2 sees this as already accomplished in the mind of God: *"The* LORD *has made known His salvation; He has revealed His righteousness in the sight of the nations."* Is it not clear that Israel will be blessed for the blessing of others? As the firstborn of the Lord (Exodus 4:22) the blessing of God bestowed on them was to go out to all the world. God's grace is channeled through Israel to the nations.

The psalm goes on to speak, in the second place, of the blessing of the Messiah's reign.

THE BLESSING OF THE MESSIAH'S REIGN (PSALM 67:3-4)

Verses 3 and 5 of Psalm 67 are identical and constitute a refrain. The longing of the redeemed in Israel in a state of blessing will draw all the nations of the world to the Lord. Hear the words of the prophet Isaiah (2:2-4): *"In the last days, the mountain of the house of the* LORD *will be established as the chief of the mountains, and will be raised above the hills; and all the nations will stream to it. And many peoples will come and say, 'Come, let us go up to the mountain of the* LORD, *to the house of the God of Jacob; that He may teach us concerning His ways, and that we may walk in His paths.' For the law will go forth from Zion, and the word of the* LORD *from Jerusalem. And He will judge between the nations, and will render decisions for many peoples; and they will hammer their swords into plowshares, and their spears into pruning hooks. Nation will not lift up sword against na-*

tion, and never again will they learn war." (Also see Zechariah 8:20-23.)

The nations will rejoice at the blessings yet to come to Israel and all the world in the reign of King Messiah. The subject of the praise of the nations will be the glory of being ruled and governed by the Messiah Himself. For the first time in the experience of the world there will be government with the strictest of equity. Messiah's shepherd care of the nations will leave nothing to be desired. Now He must overrule the nations repeatedly, but then He will guide and shepherd them. Universal blessings will attend the rule of the Messiah (Psalm 72:12-14). Praise will go forth to the Lord from every heart that is redeemed the world over, when He judges and governs righteously. How men long and groan for this now! And how blind the world is not to know that this is found in the Messiah and Saviour alone.

A girl whose blind eyes had been opened by a surgical operation delighted in the sight of her father who had a noble appearance. His every motion was watched by his fond daughter with the keenest delight. For the first time his constant tenderness and care seemed real to her. If he even looked at her kindly, it brought tears of gladness to her eyes. She said, "To think that I have had this father for these many, many years, and never knew him!" How the nations will bless the Saviour's name, for He has been near and accessible all these centuries but they never knew Him.

Last, the psalmist brings to our attention the truth of Israel's blessing and world conversion.

ISRAEL'S BLESSING AND WORLD CONVERSION (PSALM 67:5-7)

The yearning of the believing heart that God may be fully praised is again expressed in verse 5. Judging from verse 6, many have taken the occasion of the psalm to be an abundant harvest. But spiritual interpreters readily see beyond this to a time when all nations shall recognize and praise God (Leviticus 26:4). The curse will yet be removed from nature. The physical harvest is a prophecy of a greater one in the future, and a spiritual ingathering among the nations. Material prosperity will also be present (Zechariah 9:17). There will be both material and spiritual blessings (Amos 9:11-15).

The designation of God as their own God marks the blessed sense of having Him as theirs in the joy of spiritual possession. The psalm concludes with the powerful statement that God will bless Israel, and all the ends of the earth will reverence Him. The repentant Jew is the way of blessing—life from the dead for the world. The Spirit of God repeatedly reminds us that the condition for world blessing and world conversion is that Israel be blessed first. This is then a missionary psalm which looks ahead to the worldwide spread of the knowledge of God, which expects the blessing of Israel to be transmitted to the nations of the earth.

Some time ago in a public address a man spoke slurringly of foreign missions, whereupon a Jew arose and said: "Some years ago my bank sent me to look at some land in Puerto Rico. The village I visited was the nastiest, vilest little hell I ever saw. Two years ago I was sent to the same town. It was a beautiful little place, with neat houses and yards, clean streets, a pretty school for children, no vice or drunkenness in evidence, good gardens, and a church. What did it? A missionary had come there from the United States. I sought him out and gave him my check because I had never seen so much civilization accomplished in so short a time. And now, when I hear such speeches as these, I say, 'How ignorant and provincial such men are!'"

But in that day Israel will do more than merely praise the outward results of the spread of the Gospel. She will scatter abroad the Word of God herself (Isaiah 61:5-6). God always purposed a worldwide mission for His chosen nation. Through the mouth of His prophet, He said: *"The people whom I formed for Myself, will declare My praise"* (Isaiah 43:21).

8

Praying for the Peace of Jerusalem

THE GREATEST DEVOTIONAL LITERATURE in the world is to be found in the Old Testament Book of Psalms. A superficial reading of some of these songs of praise may lead one to conclude that they are separate and unrelated poems. Strictly speaking, this is not true. There are combinations of psalms and various arrangements of them. One group of psalms has been called the pilgrim songs. They are Psalms 120 through 134. They were sung as the caravans of pilgrims wended their way from different parts of the land of Canaan up to the holy city of Jerusalem for the annual festival occasions.

The third in this group, Psalm 122, reads as follows:

"A Song of Ascents, of David. I was glad when they said to me, 'Let us go to the house of the LORD*.' Our feet are standing within your gates, O Jerusalem, Jerusalem, that is built as a city that is compact together; to which the tribes go up, even the tribes of the* LORD *— an ordinance for Israel — to give thanks to the name of the* LORD*. For there thrones were set for judgment, the thrones of the house of David. Pray for the peace of Jerusalem: 'May they prosper who love you. May peace be within your walls, and prosperity within your palaces.' For the sake of my brothers and my friends, I will now say, 'May peace be within you.' For the sake of the house of the* LORD *our God I will seek your good."*

The psalm begins with an invitation to go up to the house of the Lord, then proceeds to speak of the joy of the pilgrim when his feet at last stand within the gates of the beloved city. His mind and heart turn to the prominence of the city in spiritual and in governmental matters, and in just that order. The psalm concludes with a heartfelt exhortation to pray for the peace of Jerusalem.

The exhortation of the psalmist David combines three distinct elements. The first is the command: prayer.

THE COMMAND: PRAYER

There are many voices that fill the air today, and many of them are strident as they proclaim their versions of the solution for Jerusalem's problems. The Zionist says nationalize. He seeks by every means to lay heavy emphasis on the need for a national consciousness and united action. In the case of Israel it is like carrying the proverbial coals to the proverbial Newcastle. It is like attempting to make fire hot. God Himself has set within the heart of the Jew a concern for Jerusalem and the nation which cannot be erased.

The confirmed nationalist advocates to mobilize. For him the way to accomplish the highest good for God's people is to muster the greatest forces to make the national will known and felt in the councils of the nations of the world. All Israel or Jerusalem needs is to marshal sufficient strength and prowess. The internationalist says fraternize. His method of operation is to make friends of all and forget national distinctions. This is the way Jerusalem can hope to solve her difficulties. The humanist says humanize; realize the worth of the individual man and strive for nothing more.

In the midst of this welter and confusion of tongues, the psalmist cries out to agonize. Yes, he means pray. Prayer may seem the most useless and futile of all ways of accomplishing things in our world, but it is definitely and repeatedly the way of God's appointment. All too many other methods have been introduced and tried for the benefit of Israel; this avenue of prayer, of intercession, needs to be tried now, and most desperately. How God delights to answer prayer! It is the swiftest thing known to man.

When they were putting up telegraph wires in the Shetland Islands a number of years ago, a smart businessman turned to a boy in the crowd, and said, "What a wonderful thing! When those wires are completed, you will be able to send a message through to Aberdeen, many miles away, and get an answer back in twenty minutes."

"I do not see anything wonderful in that," answered the boy.

"Do you know of anything more wonderful?" asked the surprised man.

"I should think I do," said the boy. "I have heard of people getting an answer before they sent their message."

"Why, boy, what do you mean by that? How could it be?"

"I have read in my Bible, '*It will also come to pass that before they call, I will answer; and while they are still speaking, I will hear*'" (Isaiah 65:24; see Jeremiah 51:50).

The second element in the exhortation of David is the object: peace of Jerusalem.

THE OBJECT: PEACE OF JERUSALEM

Verse 6 of Psalm 122 has beautiful plays on words. Jerusalem itself means "city of peace." Pray, says he, that her condition may tally and accord with her name. There is a play on the words "peace" and "prosperity" which are similar in sound and sense. Peace includes the ideas of welfare, prosperity, and happiness. It is not the mere physical well-being of a city, as much as that may mean, but the spiritual welfare of the individual members of the city. Jerusalem is called Salem (peace) in Psalm 76:2. God wanted His Temple a house of peace, as He made plain. David could not build the Temple because he was a man of war. Solomon, whose name means peace, had to build it.

The account is found in 1 Chronicles 22:7-10: "*And David said to Solomon, 'My son, I had intended to build a house to*

the name of the LORD *my God. But the word of the* LORD
*came to me, saying, "You have shed much blood, and have
waged great wars; you shall not build a house to My name,
because you have shed so much blood on the earth before
Me. Behold, a son shall be born to you, who shall be a man of
rest; and I will give him rest from all his enemies on every
side; for his name shall be Solomon, and I will give peace and
quiet to Israel in his days. He shall build a house for My
name, and he shall be My son, and I will be his father; and I
will establish the throne of his kingdom over Israel forever"'"*
Similarly, the Lord wants peace of mind and heart in His city
of peace, the city of the Prince of Peace. How God desires
the peace of the individual soul!

During the World's Columbian Exposition in Chicago in
1893 there was one place in the Tiffany exhibit that one could
seldom get near because of the great crowd gathered around
it. Dr. Torrey said he was there many times but never could
get at the place. He always had to stand on tiptoe and look
over the heads of the crowd. What were they looking at?
Nothing but a cone of purple velvet revolving on an axis, and
toward the apex of the cone a large, beautiful diamond of
almost priceless worth. It was well worth looking at.

But Torrey never recalled the scene but what the thought
came to him that the single soul of the most ragged pauper on
the streets, of the most degraded woman, of the most ignorant boy or girl, is of infinitely more value in God's sight than
ten thousand gems like that. In order to procure peace for
them all, the Lord Jesus suffered the death of Calvary. He
longs that Jerusalem may enter into that peace, and such
should be the object of our praying.

Finally, the last important element in the words of David is
the promise: prosperity of the godly.

THE PROMISE: PROSPERITY OF THE GODLY

The Hebrew word *prosper* means to be secure, at rest, tran-
quil. The promise is to those who love Jerusalem. The motive

in the ministry of prayer for Israel and Jerusalem must be unselfish love and concern for their eternal good. As God said to Abraham, "I will bless those that bless you," so here it is that they might *"'prosper who love you'"* (Psalm 122:6). Those who see the motive here as mere selfishness fail to realize that if Jerusalem is loved for one's own sake it would not be loving her at all. The reason that prompted David's prayers for Zion was love for the brethren, the friends of Jerusalem, and the house of the Lord. There is no doubt of the soul prosperity that the Lord can give when we carry through His purposes. The house of Obed-Edom was blessed because of the Ark of the Lord, for which he made a place in his home.

When we care for the things of God, He will care for our things. Sad to say, there are those who hate Zion (Psalm 129:5). Their number seems to increase by bounds. And they are traveling on rapidly to their doom. They little realize how they incur the wrath of Almighty God upon them in their blind and satanic fury against the people of God. There is a Jewish proverb: "None ever took a stone out of the Temple, but the dust did fly into his eyes." The meaning is clear: no one touches Israel for good without the notice of God, and no one touches them for harm without heaping upon himself wrath in the Day of Judgment for opposing the evident and declared will of God. Remember, God has joined together giving and receiving, scattering and increasing, sowing and reaping, praying and prospering.

We could multiply the experiences of godly men and women who have proved the truth of this blessed exhortation and promise. They have put God to the test and found He meant every word He said. Let us, then, by the grace and help of God, obey the command to pray and realize thus the blessing that flows immediately from it.

Part 4

ISRAEL IN THE GOSPELS

9

"Salvation Is from the Jews"

NONE OF THE INTERVIEWS which Jesus the Messiah of Israel had when He was ministering on earth was without significance or deep interest. This is certainly true of the encounter He had with the woman of Samaria recorded in chapter 4 of the gospel of John. She had come seeking for physical water to quench her physical thirst, but the Lord Jesus Christ pointed to Himself as the unfailing Source of spiritual refreshing and spiritual life. When the Lord laid His finger on the spiritual cancer in her life, she used diversive tactics to shift the spotlight from herself to others.

The account reads in part: *"The woman said to Him, 'Sir, I perceive that You are a prophet. Our fathers worshiped in this mountain; and you people say that in Jerusalem is the place where men ought to worship.' Jesus said to her, 'Woman, believe Me, an hour is coming when neither in this mountain, nor in Jerusalem, shall you worship the Father. You worship that which you do not know; we worship that which we know; for salvation is from the Jews. But an hour is coming, and now is, when the true worshipers shall worship the Father in spirit and truth; for such people the Father seeks to be His worshipers. God is Spirit; and those who worship Him must worship in spirit and truth.' The woman said to Him, 'I know that Messiah is coming (He who is called Christ); when that One comes, He will declare all things to us.' Jesus said to her, 'I who speak to you am He'"* (4:19-26).

When Christ indicated that the Samaritans knew not what they worshiped, He referred to the fact that the Samaritans rejected the prophets and the writings of the Old Testament. They were thus deprived of the additional and fuller revelation of God given there. The difference in Jewish and Samaritan worship lay not in difference of place of worship but in the object of worship. The Samaritan religion, even after the original elements of idolatry (2 Kings 17:33, 41) had been removed, was a perverted religion. The five books of Moses, which they had in a poor text, were not clarified nor illuminated by the clearer revelations God gave the prophets. But the Messiah of Israel declared that the Jews knew what they worshiped, for they had the full testimony of God's revelation in the Old Testament. The Jews know their God, for salvation comes from them. God's redemptive program was intended and is for the whole world (John 3:16-17), but it comes from (out of) the Jews.

What did Christ mean when He made the sweeping and vastly important statement, "salvation is from the Jews"? He was here comprehending in small compass the whole range of redemptive truth. Salvation is indeed from the Jews in a threefold way. In the first place, salvation is from the Jews in its preparation.

FROM THE JEWS

All the preparatory steps and stages of God's redemptive scheme were laid in the realm of Israel's spiritual life. Salvation was promised to Abraham and his descendants. God solemnly promised to Abraham that in him, in his seed which is the Messiah, would all the families of the earth be blessed. This same covenant commitment was ratified and remade with Isaac and Jacob and their descendants (Genesis 12:3; 18:18; 22:18; 26:4).

The salvation of the Lord was portrayed by Moses in the tabernacle with its furniture. The altar of burnt offering meant the coming Messiah would be the believer's justification. The laver spoke of Messiah our sanctification. The table of showbread pointed to Christ our food. The candlestick was the indication of Messiah as our light. The altar of incense spoke eloquently of Christ our Intercessor. The veil into the holiest of all declared the Messiah as our access to God. The Ark of the Covenant preached the truth of Christ as our Representative in the presence of God.

Not only did the Mosaic tabernacle picture salvation in its preparatory stages, but the priesthood was vocal with its exhibition of the truth that the coming Messiah was to be the High Priest to make sacrifice for sin and to make prevailing intercession for His own. Furthermore, the very sacrifices all set Him forth as the perfect One in His person and work. The whole burnt offering meant to tell us that He offered Himself unreservedly and obediently to carry out the full will of the Father. The meal offering pictured Him as the blemishless and stainless One in His perfect and ideal humanity. The peace offering could mean nothing other than He was to accomplish the procuring of our peace with God from whom we, as sinners, were all so grievously estranged.

The sin offering took into account that the Messiah would die for the sin nature of man which is under the curse of God and condemned utterly. The trespass offering had in view the restoration of that which has been lost through transgression, and the Messiah in His death restored that which He took not away. Who will dare to say that Moses spoke not gloriously of the Messiah yet to come? But the end is not yet, for the Hebrew prophets are full of glowing predictions of the Messiah's divine nature and finished work. Isaiah speaks of His virgin birth from a maiden in the house of David. The future rule of the King of Israel, as well as the path of sorrow and suffering necessary to that goal, are also vividly presented (Isaiah 7:14; 9:5-6; 53).

Jeremiah pointed to the One who is David's righteous Branch through whom justice and righteousness will be meted out in the land, whose name is the Lord our Righteousness (23:5-6). Ezekiel delighted to speak of the righteous and

tender Shepherd of Israel who will gather the outcasts of
Israel and the dispersed of Judah and care for their every
need (34:11-16). The prophet Daniel in Babylonian exile
looked far into the future day and predicted the very time of
the Messiah's coming for the salvation of the world (9:24-26).
The message of Micah included even the very place where the
Saviour was to be born into the world: Bethlehem of Judea
(5:2). Malachi unerringly pointed out the forerunner of the
Messiah, as well as the coming of the Redeemer Himself to
His temple (3:1). The expected Messiah and Saviour and His
salvation were the dominant notes and themes in the predictions of the Old Testament prophets.

A Hyde Park orator was denouncing the feeble efforts of
the Jews to resist the Roman oppression in the first century of
the Christian era, and suggested that if they had appealed
more to the sword and less to the sacred writings, they might
have fared much better. One in the crowd asked, "But where
are the Romans today?" "Nowhere," was the quick answer.
"And where are the Jews today?" "Everywhere," was the sar-
castic but true reply to the evident appreciation of the
hearers. Yes, it was those sacred writings which indicated the
preservation of the nation and people of Israel and also
foretold of the glorious coming salvation to be brought to
them by the Messiah, the Son of David.

In the second place, salvation is from the Jews in its presentation.

AMONG THE JEWS

All too often it is overlooked that the Jews had an equally
large and important portion in the presentation of God's
salvation, as in the preparation. You do not need to read very
far into the New Testament before you are aware that the
coming Saviour was heralded by a Jewish forerunner, John
the Baptizer (Matthew 3:1-3). In true Old Testament prophetic form this man of God summoned Israel to repent and
turn to God in preparation for the soon approach of the

Messiah. Then when the Saviour did come incarnate in the human family, it was to a Jewish virgin that He turned to find His parental abode. He was born of a Jewish virgin of the royal house of David in the truly Jewish city of Bethlehem of Judah (Luke 1:26-33; Galatians 4:4).

He observed the regulations of the Law and the feasts of the Hebrew Scriptures. Also, He was announced to the Jews. He made known that He had come to Israel as her Messiah and King. He sent His disciples to minister and preach to the lost sheep of the house of Israel (Matthew 2:1-2; 10:5-6; 21:9-11). Finally, when we are thinking of the presentation of salvation or its manifestation, we need only be reminded that salvation was finished by the King of the Jews. The super-scription over His cross as He died, proclaimed to all men everywhere that He was the King of the Jews as He paid the ransom for our sins (Matthew 27:37; John 19:19). Even when opposing men wanted this changed, it could not be altered. Truly, salvation is of the Jews in its manifestation in a Jewish environment with Jewish participants, centering in the Jewish Messiah and King.

Finally, salvation is from the Jews in its propagation.

THROUGH THE JEWS

Not all are aware that the first preachers of the Messianic message and salvation were Jewish disciples. The Messiah chose certain men to proclaim abroad the message of His appearance and the gracious purpose of God. These men were all to a man of the Jewish household of faith (Matthew 10:2-6; Luke 10:1). In fact, the Saviour made it plain that they were to direct their ministry to Israel alone. From the very first the blessed message of God was opposed by the ungodly who heard it. In those days the word was often sealed by the blood of the witness. We must never forget that the first martyrs of the faith were Jewish: Stephen (Acts 7:59-60) and James, the brother of John (Acts 12:1-2). The apostles who laid the early groundwork for the spread of the truth were Jewish apostles (Acts 2:14; 10:25-43). The apostles Peter and Paul were from Israel. Thus from start to finish the great work of salvation was permeated with the presence of Jews. Our Lord spoke meaningful words when He said: "Salvation is from the Jews."

Because salvation is of and from the Jews does not mean that all Jews or any Jew is thereby saved and in possession of that salvation. It is a Jewish household of faith, but, sad to say, the majority of them have vacated the house. A prominent rabbi said recently, "We have given the world their religions, but have none ourselves." The reason is clear: they are seeking to establish their own righteousness and salvation which God Himself has provided.

A minister was going along the road one day when he saw a man working in a field. He could see the land was not of much value, so he said: "Sir, your land is not very productive; is it?" "No, it's just like self-righteousness," the man plainly stated. "Indeed, how's that?" asked the interested preacher. The man answered, "The more a man has of it, the poorer he is." Give up your self-righteousness and trust the Messiah and Saviour and His divine righteousness.

Part 5

ISRAEL IN THE EPISTLES

10

A Love for Israel

*"I am telling the truth in Christ, I am not lying, my
conscience bearing me witness in the Holy Spirit, that
I have great sorrow and unceasing grief in my heart.
For I could wish that I myself were accursed, separated from Christ for the sake of my brethren, my
kinsmen according to the flesh, who are Israelites, to
whom belongs the adoption as sons and the glory and
the covenants and the giving of the Law and the temple service and the promises, whose are the fathers,
and from whom is the Christ according to the flesh,
who is over all, God blessed forever. Amen."*

(Romans 9:1-5)

MANY TERM CHAPTERS 9-11 of Romans parenthetical, but
they cannot be considered such if the argument of the epistle
is really understood. The great truth of justification by faith
and sanctification by faith are here set alongside of the Old
Testament promises and covenants to Israel. Will they stand?
These three chapters show that they not only stand, but they
harmonize with the whole redemptive plan of God. Nor are
these chapters parenthetical in the life and experience of
Paul. In fact, they are central; they reveal what were the inner
springs, motives, and impulses of his ministry. Paul speaks
very intimately of his life and ministry in the second letter to
the Corinthians, but no more so than here in this portion of

Romans. At the beginning of each of these three chapters the person and heart of the apostle are prominent. The first five verses of chapter 9 serve as an introductory word to the whole section. Here we find Paul's pain and his passion as well as Israel's privileges. Through it all there flames forth the love and passion of Paul for his own kinsmen, for Israel, for the Jews. In this short passage we find the sorrow of Paul.

THE SORROW OF PAUL (ROMANS 9:1-2)

Note how strongly Paul affirms his sorrow in the first verse. He was regarded by his countrymen and coreligionists as a traitor and enemy, so he states his sincerity (Acts 21:33; 22:22; 25:24). Paul really makes a threefold oath, so greatly is he moved by his sorrow. (Notice that he does not mention the cause of his sorrow: the lost condition of Israel; it is too great a burden on the heart even to be uttered.) His unceasing pain is like angina pectoris, a consuming grief. This grief and sorrow of the apostle are present at the moment of greatest joy in contemplating the blessings of salvation (cf. Romans 8:31-39). At the moment of highest joy in the Lord for himself, he is conscious of the deepest pain and anguish for Israel, his "kinsmen according to the flesh."

Paul could have easily excused himself of interest in them by pleading (1) his commission to the office of apostle to the Gentiles. He could have said his mind and heart and energies and thoughts were so occupied with other fields and with the prosecution of the work of the Gospel among the Gentiles and Gentile believers that he had no time to think or to sorrow for Israel. But he never did make such a statement nor intimate it. He says plainly the opposite here. He could have advanced another excuse: (2) their continued and determined opposition to him and his ministry (Lystra and Derbe, cf. also 1 Thessalonians 2:16). But Paul was always so occupied with Christ that he never lent his great heart to petty quibblings, but to passionate love for them and sorrow on their behalf.

It is told of John Vassar that he had many remarkable experiences in his visitation work. In one village an Irish woman heard that he was distributing tracts and speaking with people as he had opportunity to do so, and she said: "If he comes to my door I will not treat him kindly." The next day he rang her door bell, and on recognizing him, she slammed the door in his face. He then sat down on the doorstep and sang:

> But drops of grief can ne'er repay
> The debt of love I owe;
> Here, Lord, I give myself away,
> 'Tis all that I can do.

She afterward confessed that it was those "drops of grief" that reached her heart and led her to place her faith in Christ. Paul had many a drop of grief in his heart for Israel and how he longed that it might lead them to see Him who shed more than drops of grief for them, yes, even drops of precious and divine blood.

THE SELF-SACRIFICE OF PAUL (ROMANS 9:3)

In these first five verses of Romans 9 and especially verse 3, men have spent more time, and perhaps too much time, on the bare matter of language, and not enough on the passion and feeling of the apostle portrayed throughout this passage and section. He is saying he could wish, if it were possible but it is not (Psalm 49:7-8), that he were accursed eternally from Christ for the sake of Israel. Anathema is that which originally signified the act of depositing gifts in temples which were then irrevocable. It came to mean anything irrevocably and irretrievably devoted to destruction. Paul knew what this would mean for an Israelite under the curses of the Law of Moses (cf. Deuteronomy 28:16-19). He also knew what that would mean to a believer to be delivered over to Satan for the destruction of the flesh, and excommunication from the fellowship of fellow saints in the Lord.

Here it is not just anathema from the Jewish congregation or the Christian assembly and fellowship, but anathema from Christ, which is eternal perdition. This is not the desire of one tired of a ruined and miserable life, but one who was enjoying the joy of the Lord as the very chief of the apostles. Some interpret it to mean before his conversion ("I had wished"). But did Paul seek his people's conversion to Christ before he was saved himself? The record in Acts makes it clear that he did all in his power to keep them from that very course.

Some try to soften the language. It cannot be done. Paul was in dead earnest, as the entire passage so clearly reveals. Note Moses in Exodus 32:32 (probably only physical death is meant). Note also the love of Jeremiah and the prophets for Israel. But these do not quite approximate the passion here. It is safe to say no one knew better than Paul what it meant to be saved from the depths of sin (read his own words in 1 Timothy 1:15), nor what it was to dwell daily in the heights of salvation joy in Christ (Philippians 1:21), yet Paul was ready and willing to give up all this if Israel might know Christ by faith. Paul was willing to give up all that was dear to him naturally in Judaism for the excellency of the knowledge of Christ (Philippians 3:1-11), and now he was willing to give up all that was dear to him spiritually in Christ for his own kinsmen. And these were not rash words, nor indeed cold intellectualism, but warm and burning and glowing and consuming passion.

What fellowship he was having in this with our blessed Lord Jesus Christ who said (Matthew 23:37); who did (Philippians 2:5-11); who died (Galatians 3:13-14)! No wonder Dorner called it "a spark from the fire of Christ's substitutionary love." It was much more than mere patriotism. If we view it thus, we have missed the great and chief point of it all. Patriotism in and of itself is not necessarily Christian. True, the spiritual believer, who is commanded to be subject to the higher power (Romans 13:1-7), will be patriotic, but patriotism per se is not primarily Christian. Most of the pagan countries of ancient times revealed unsurpassed patriotism. Certainly Paul was revealing more than this. It is Christian passion for the lost. Such passion should be extensive enough to include the whole world, but it need not thereby lose its intensity. Such true, intense love always seeks to suffer in the place of its object. Think of how that passion moved him and shaped the course of his ministry.

THE SOVEREIGN LOVE OF GOD (ROMANS 9:4-5)

If we stop at verse 3 and fail to catch the force of verses 4 and 5 of Romans 9 we have lost a good deal of the apostle's reasoning. By the catalog in verses 4 and 5 Paul is enumerating God's tokens of love to Israel and thus saying that he must love where God loves. Every privilege noted is a token, clear and manifest, that God loves Israel and has a passion for them. God's love for them is a full and gracious one (cf. Deuteronomy 7:7-8). It followed them all the days of their history and continues even to this hour (Deuteronomy 32:10; Isaiah 49:16; 63:9; Jeremiah 31:3; Zechariah 2:8). It was and is strong and intense (Matthew 9:36; Isaiah 62:6-7). Paul says that if God has singled them out by His overflowing love, then he, too, shall love them with a passion unsurpassed by any other man.

There is a story of a poor woman from the slums of London who took her first trip to the seashore and looked for the first time at the ocean. Tears were streaming down her face. Someone standing by her asked why she was crying. "Oh, it is so wonderful," she said, "to see something that there is enough of." So it is with God's love; there is enough of it and more than enough for all, and for Israel surely. Remember that the passion for Israel was not just some mental or emotional peculiarity of the apostle Paul; he caught the fire from the heart of God! And he not only loved Israel as a whole, but the individual Jew! Can we afford to do otherwise?

11

A Prayer for Israel

IN ROMANS 10, as well as in the preceding and the following chapters, Paul begins with a personal word: *"Brethren, my heart's desire and my prayer to God for them is for their salvation"* (v. 1). Again he reveals his attitude toward Israel. The Scriptures reveal two ways of praying in relation to Israel: for Israel (Paul in Romans 10:1), and against Israel (Elijah in Romans 11:2). That the latter way is displeasing to God can be seen from the narrative in 1 Kings 19, the answer of God to Elijah, and the place in which Elijah found himself at the time. He was in the place of fear and cowardice, in the place of unbelief, in the place of shortsightedness (he thought there was only one worshiper of God in Israel, but there were 7,000 others, which is a difference), and in the place of disobedience (God asked him, "What are you doing here, Elijah?"). If we would be pleasing to God in our prayer relationship to Israel, we must be sure, then, that it is for Israel and not against her.

Paul gives the three elements that should enter into the proper prayer for Israel: concern, fervency, and salvation.

THE PRAYER OF CONCERN

Paul at the very outset of Chapter 10 expresses again (as in 9:1-3) his state of anxiety and solicitude for Israel. He is full of desire, concern, and interest for them. This is much more

than that tolerance of which many speak and for which many
are laboring. Tolerance is to be commended, but it is insuffi-
cient when praying for Israel. This is also much more than
sympathy or pity, which may be the beginning or start of a
real solicitous concern for Israel, but they surely are not that
concern itself. When Paul says it is his heart's desire, he
means it is that thing in which the heart would experience full
satisfaction, in which it could complacently rest. It was more
than a professional interest, or an obligatory interest, or an
intellectual interest. It was such a heartfelt, earnest interest
that his heart could find no satisfaction or complacency in
anything else when thinking of Israel.

Think of Nero as he sat in all his pomp and glory as the
conqueror of the world. It is said that the porticoes of his
palace were a mile long, the walls of mother-of-pearl and
ivory, the ceilings arranged to shower fragrant perfumes
upon his guests. His crown was worth half a million dollars,
his mules were shod with silver, he fished with hooks of gold,
a thousand carriages attended him when he traveled. His
wardrobe contained clothing in such abundance that he never
wore a garment a second time; wealth and riches were there
indeed. Yet he was not a satisfied man, because he knew not
God. His arm had conquered, but his heart remained unsatisfied.

Paul knew what this satisfaction meant, for he had it in
Christ. But when he viewed Israel in its unsaved state he was
unsatisfied and he found his heart without complacent rest
for their condition. Notice three indications of that deep
solicitude for them. (1) When he had to state clearly the
truths of the Gospel with no discrimination for either Jew or
Gentile, he always tried to allay their opposition and enmity
by reaffirming his interest in and love for them. (2) When he
stated their case and position, he was careful not to exagger-
ate their condition (how different from the practice of many
in our day), and he tried to credit them and commend where
possible. (3) He made it plain that he did not delight in their
plight or in the contemplation of the evils to befall them.

Before real prayer can be made, then, there must be godly and genuine concern.

A personal friend told of a woman who came to him and asked for his prayers for her wayward boy. When he asked her if she had prayed for her son and had held onto God in his behalf, she said, "In a way I have." Then our friend with great feeling said, "My dear lady, ask God to place that child, whom you bore so long under your heart, upon your heart!" How can anyone pray earnestly for that which is not a burden on the heart? Before we pray for Israel, we must be sure that our impulse is solicitude for their condition.

The Prayer of Fervency

Because the apostle's heart's desire was not merely an external thing, he gave fervent and ardent expression to it in supplication. He vocalized that desire in prayer to God. The apostle had a heart's desire. What did he do about it? He preached to them; he prayed for them; he persuaded others to become interested in them. His was interested prayer, intelligent prayer, and intercessory prayer. His interest was not shallow; he knew the facts of the case. His prayer was not selfish in the least; he wanted the benefit to accrue to them.

The Scriptures give a picture of supplication in the case of the woman of Shunem who came to Elisha to plead for her son. We have all heard men, and they are godly men too, pray for every nation under heaven, from the benighted Hottentot of Africa to the demon-possessed Brahmin of India to the savage cannibals of the South Sea Islands, but how often do we hear prayer for Israel and for their salvation in Christ? Where does the root of the trouble lie? Is it not that the heart's desire is lacking so that there can be no expression of it? Men may hinder other efforts on their behalf (note the times that Paul was hindered in preaching to them), but they cannot hinder prayer. God needs more men and women with a burning desire for Israel to supplicate for them.

The incident is told that during the troubled days in Scotland, when the papal court and the aristocracy were arrayed against the Reformation in that country, and the cause of Protestant Christianity was in dire danger, late one night John Knox was seen to leave his study and to go from his home down into an enclosure at the rear of it. He was followed by a friend. After a few moments his voice was heard in prayer. In another moment the sounds were audible words, and the burning petition went up from his agonizing soul to heaven, "O Lord, give me Scotland, or I die!" Then there followed a pause, and again the petition poured forth, "O Lord, give me Scotland, or I die!" Once more all was quiet, and then with even greater intensity, the thrice-uttered intercession struggled forth: "O Lord, give me Scotland, or I die!" And God did give Knox Scotland in spite of Mary, Cardinal Beatoun, and their followers. The hour and the need call for just such supplicators for God's chosen people, Israel.

THE PRAYER FOR SALVATION

The burden of Paul's prayer and its object are not small. They are nothing more nor less than the salvation of Israel. His prayer is "for them," for Israel who have been the subject of the letter in chapter 9.

Paul knew full well (1) the need of it. Here was a people with zeal for God, not irreligious, but deeply religious. Yet theirs was a zeal which took no account of the righteousness of God which He had provided in Christ Jesus the Lord. Hence they labored and sought incessantly to establish a righteousness of their own with the result that they did not submit themselves to the righteousness of God and the plan He had prepared for them and for all the world. How they needed to be saved!

Paul also knew (2) the possibility of their salvation. Bengel has well said, "Paul would not have prayed if they had been absolutely reprobate." There was and is a definite possibility of it.

He knew (3) the ample provision for it. He says: *"For there is no distinction between Jew and Greek; for the same Lord is Lord of all, abounding in riches for all who call upon Him; for, 'Whoever will call upon the name of the Lord will be saved'"* (Romans 10:12-13).

He foresaw also (4) the glory of it. The glory was to be for Christ, because he knew the blessed Saviour wanted to see of the travail of His soul for them and be satisfied (Isaiah 53:11). Glory to the world, for it would indeed be "life from the dead" (Romans 11:15). No doubt many Christian people are praying for Israel in her time of trial, but are they praying for her salvation or merely the cessation of her trials? Why ask for the lesser when the greater is possible?

It is said of Theodore Monod, the famous French preacher, that he was telling his younger brother about Christ healing blind Bartimaeus. He asked the boy, "And what would you have asked of the Lord Jesus if you had been blind?" "Oh," answered the lad with face aglow and eyes shining, "I would have asked Him for a nice little dog with a collar and string to lead me about." How many ask for the blind man's dog instead of the seeing man's eyes when they pray for Israel.

Let us pray earnestly and effectively for God's people, Israel. Let us not limit the Holy One of Israel.

12

A Hope for Israel

"I say then, God has not rejected His people, has He? May it never be! For I too am an Israelite, a descendant of Abraham, of the tribe of Benjamin"
(Romans 11:11)

IT IS THE CONFIRMED belief of many, contrary to the Scriptures, that there is no hope nor prospect for God's people, Israel. They believe God has completely and finally cast her off. A letter addressed to the editor of a religious weekly concerning an article on the Jew said: "But the Bible, Old as well as New, more powerfully condemns the Jew than even a Hitler or a Roman did. And what is more, this eternal condemnation has already rested on him for 2000 years and more, and will so rest, we may well judge, to the end of time. When you quote God's Word to the effect that in Abraham shall all families of the earth be blessed and that a curse shall rest upon any who curse him, you quote a Scripture that was completely fulfilled in the words from the cross 'It is finished.'" If God is not faithful to His promises to Israel, will He be any more so to His promises to His Church? If the failure of Israel is argued, can it not be equally argued that the Church has miserably failed God also?

The prospect of Israel is not extinction. With such determined opposition from every side and from such inveterate enemies it appears as though the only prospect possible for Israel is their annihilation or extinction. But the prophet Jeremiah refutes this for all time: *"Thus says the* LORD, *who gives the sun for light by day, and the fixed order of the moon and the stars for light by night, who stirs up the sea so that its waves roar; the* LORD *of hosts is His name: 'If this fixed order departs from before Me,' declares the* LORD, *'then the off- spring of Israel also shall cease from being a nation before Me forever.' Thus says the* LORD, *'If the heavens above can be measured, and the foundations of the earth searched out below, then I will also cast off all the offspring of Israel for all that they have done,' declares the* LORD" (31:35-37).

Israel is the burning bush that was not consumed, not con- sumed because the Lord was in the bush (Jeremiah 30:11). Nor is her prospect Zionism. Much hope has been placed in Zionism and much effort placed in it. The recent years of the establishment of the State of Israel have seen renewed energy on every hand. But Zionism has undergone many failures, and will see many more. The national prospect of Israel is not in the patronage of governments. Men and the arm of flesh will always fail. Her prospect is not realized in these directions.

God has not cast Israel away for all time and given her promises totally and finally to any other nation, or even to the Church. Someone has well said, "While Japheth is en- titled to share the tent with Shem, he has no right to steal the tent and turn Shem out, robbed of his promises and his inher- itance."

Israel's prospect is not in extinction, nor in the arm of flesh, nor in Zionism, nor in friendly gestures from kindly disposed governments, but this does not mean God has cast her off. Is there a prospect for her? Does hope yet remain for her? In the much neglected chapter 11 of Romans this is fully answered.

Paul proves conclusively that there is a prospect for Israel by three irrefutable arguments: (1) Paul himself in the past, (2) the remnant in the present, and (3) all Israel in the future.

Paul Himself in the Past (Romans 11:1)

If God had completely cast off His people after the cruci-fixion of Christ, then how is it that Paul is saved himself? Note the connection of 11:1 with the last verse of Romans 10, where it is stated that God is stretching out His hands all the day long to a disobedient and obstinate people. If such is the case, if He be pleading with them daily and now, how then can anyone claim that God has cast off His people?

Place Romans 11:1 in syllogistic form (as a friend has done) to see how impossible it is of being the truth that God has cast away His people and is "through with the Jews." The syllogism could read thus:

> God is through with the Jew.
> I, Paul, am a Jew.
> Therefore, God is through with me.

But this verse proves not only that an individual can be saved, but that like Paul, Israel will be saved. In 1 Timothy 1:16 Paul indicates that God manifested His grace, His loving-kindness, and His mercy to him while he was yet a persecutor, injurious and blasphemous, because God wanted to show forth in Christ all His long-suffering for an example to those that would afterward believe on the Lord Jesus Christ unto eternal life.

This passage means that Paul in his conversion in the past is a picture and an assurance that God will save Israel in the future. There are definite similarities: Israel and Paul were both unbelieving, fanatical, ignorant of God's righteousness, and zealous; both will have the vision of the glorified and ascended Christ as the cause of their acceptance of Him by faith; the ministry of both is to all the nations of the earth. (See Isaiah 2:1-4; Micah 4:1-5; Zechariah 8:20-23.) How can it be said that God has cast off His people when Paul was saved and Israel will be saved after this same type?

THE REMNANT IN THE PRESENT (ROMANS 11:2-24)

How can it be said God has cast away His people when the remnant of the present is considered? The remnant now, as in other ages, proves that the apostasy of Israel is never a complete one. From the times of greatest apostasy God has always had a remnant in Israel, whether in Elijah's time, in Isaiah's time, or in the time of our Lord Jesus Christ (Simeon and Anna). Some interpret verses 7 to 10 as stating Israel is cast off for all time. But surely all the passage teaches is that there is a remnant in the midst of seeming universal apostasy. Their fall is not final. No, its purpose was to bring salvation to the Gentiles so that they would provoke Israel to jealousy. If God wants them to be provoked to jealousy, surely He has not cast them off forever.

Over a quarter of a century ago a Russian Jew of great learning named Joseph Rabbinowitz was sent to Palestine by the Jews to buy land for them. He went to Jerusalem. One day he went up on the Mount of Olives to rest. Someone had told him to take a New Testament as the best guidebook about Jerusalem. The only Christ he had known was the Christ of the Greek and Roman churches, who were his persecutors and the persecutors of his people. But as he read the New Testament he became acquainted with the real Christ of whom the Old Testament Scriptures had foretold, and his heart grew warm. he looked off toward Calvary and thought: *Why is it that my people are persecuted and cast out?* And his conviction gave the answer: *It must be because we have put to death our Messiah.* He lifted his eyes to that Messiah and said: "My Lord and my God." He came down from the mount a disciple of the Lord Jesus Christ. He went home to Russia and erected a synagogue for the Jews, over the door of which was written: "Let all the house of Israel know that God hath made that same Jesus whom ye have crucified, both Lord and Christ." He was one of the many present remnant of Israel, which proves conclusively and better than words that God has not cast away His people.

ALL ISRAEL IN THE FUTURE (ROMANS 11:25-27)

Not only does Paul's conversion prove that God is not through with the Jew, but the conversion of the remnant does also. But more than that, the blessed prospect beyond us proves it without a shadow of a doubt. For then God will be dealing with Israel in a national manner again. Israel knows they have a hope: their national anthem is "The Hope." What that hope is can be found in the Scriptures which tell of a returning and reigning Messiah (Zechariah 12:10; Isaiah 24:23); a restored nation (Jeremiah 23:3-4); a regenerated people (Ezekiel 36:22-32 and Isaiah 66:8, 10), but first there must be the transaction of Ezekiel 20:38; the ratified new covenant (Jeremiah 31:31-34); the reception of the outpoured Spirit (Joel 2:28-29); the renovated earth (Isaiah 35:1-10); the rebuilt temple, the reinstituted sacrifices and feasts, and redivided land (Ezekiel 40 ff. and 45:18; 47:13-23; Zechariah 14:16 ff.). These are Israel's promises of hope, her prospects for the glorious future. She has the promise of being grafted into her own olive tree: restoration to blessing. It will be life from the dead, as with Jonah and his preaching: conversion of the whole great city. The blindness of the Jews is only partial and temporary, proving that God has not cast them off. They will yet herald abroad the truth of the Lord Jesus Christ.

Some years ago a very significant event took place in a city in our own country. A certain elevated part of the city was recognized by a real estate firm as destined to become the most fashionable part of that area. A little church building had been erected there and a mission church established. The members of this church worshiped their Lord with great enthusiasm and fervor. As costly homes were built near the church, the owners finally became disturbed by the singing. These ultra-fashionable people said: "It won't do; they disturb the quiet of our homes with their enthusiasm." They appointed a committee to go to the city council with a petition and have the church declared a nuisance. They brought the petition to a Jew, having no doubt that he would be the first to sign it. To their surprise he pushed the petition away from him and said, "I cannot sign it. If I believed as do these Christians that my Messiah had come, I would shout it from every housetop of Richmond, and nobody could stop me." Thank God, Israel will yet believe and will yet tell the glorious story.

Let us not attempt to shorten the arm of God or His good promises for the blessed prospect of Israel. Let us pray for the hastening of that blessed time that is known to God. It is known that the treasury doors of banks are able to resist almost any destructive agent that would try to open them. The lock and bolt work is mounted on the inside of the door. The bolts are controlled by two keyless combination locks, and in addition there is a time lock which prevents the door from being opened except at the determined time. This time lock of the Jew defined in Scripture in comparatively definite terms will be opened by God and no man will be able to close it. Then will begin the fulfillment of all concerning her which the Lord has promised. Be assured that God has much in prospect for His ancient people, Israel.

13

The Mystery of Israel's Blindness

THE MEANINGS OF MYSTERY, ISRAEL, AND BLINDNESS

ONE OF THE MOST interesting and profitable studies in the entire Word of God is that of the mysteries of God. We should be well acquainted with them, moreover, because the apostle Paul says that as ministers of Christ we are also the stewards of the mysteries of God. Before we attempt any discussion of this subject, let us first define our terms and make some distinctions pertinent to the matter at hand.

The word *mystery* (*musterion*) has a far different meaning in Scripture than the one in common use. It was first employed in the ancient pagan religions to denote the secret rites and ceremonies known only to those who had already been initiated into the cult. The main objective of these rites was to secure for the adherents of the religion a blessed immortality with their deity as well as present mystic union.[1]

Although this word is used seventy-seven times in the New Testament (but never in the Old Testament), it never bears the meaning that it did for the ancient pagan religions. In the New Testament it refers to a truth once hidden but now made known by a revelation from God. In fact, the terms "mystery" and "revelation" are correlative. Paul defines the term in Romans 16:25-26, stating that it is something kept

---

[1] D. M. Edwards, "Mystery," in *International Standard Bible Encyclopedia*, 3:2104.

"secret for long ages past, but now is manifested, and by the Scriptures of the prophets, according to the commandment of the eternal God."

In Ephesians 3:3-6 the apostle refers to the truth of the Church as that which in other ages was not made known unto the sons of men, but is now revealed unto God's holy apostles and prophets by His Spirit. The subject of our study is "The Mystery of Israel's Blindness" because these are the words employed by the Scriptures in speaking of this mystery and because I can see no immediate connection between the title and the specific field of the mystery if I were to call it, as does Dr. Ironside, "The Mystery of the Olive Tree."[2]

Next the term *Israel* must be defined. Such a discussion may seem unnecessary to some, but after reading work after work where Israel and the Church were spoken of and referred to as one and the same body, I have concluded that a complete definition will not be out of place. *Israel* is used in Scripture in several ways. It was first given to Jacob on that memorable night when he wrestled with God and prevailed. Scriptures use the term when speaking of all the descendants of Jacob or the twelve tribes. This is more particularly true of the time prior to the division of the Solomonic kingdom. With the breaking off of the ten tribes from Rehoboam, the term is applied to them as the kingdom of Israel.

Finally, it is the designation of those believers in Christ who are the natural descendants of Abraham. Here a distinction must be made. It is proper to speak of believing Jews and believing Gentiles as Abraham's spiritual seed (so Paul designates them in Galatians 3), but spiritual Israelites are believing Jews only. The difficulty in many cases begins with the misinterpretation of Romans 9:6 and Galatians 6:16, with the result that we have writers speaking of Israel as "his people, his Church, the recipient of his revelations, through whom he would instruct and save the world,"[3] and referring to the

---

[2] H. A. Ironside, *The Mysteries of God* (New York: Loizeaux, 1943), p. 40.
[3] R. V. Foster, *A Commentary on the Epistle to the Romans* (Nashville: Cumberland Presby. Publ., 1891), p. 307.

Church as "a new and larger Israel, gathered not from among the Jews only, but from among all nations."[4]

Upon examining Romans 9 it can easily be seen that when Paul declares, *"For they are not all Israel who are descended from Israel"* (Romans 9:6), he is not speaking of a distinction between Israel and the Church or between Gentile Christians and Jewish unbelievers. He is rather distinguishing between those in the nation Israel who are unbelievers, Abraham's natural seed, and those of Israel who are believers, the spiritual seed of Abraham. The Gentiles or the Church are here nowhere in view.

In Galatians 6:16 the apostle concludes his message: *"And those who will walk by this rule, peace and mercy be upon them, and upon the Israel of God."* Sanday and Headlam are of the opinion that Paul is using the terms here "metaphorically of Christians."[5] I agree rather with Ellicott who doubts that this terminology could be applied to Christians in general. It is used of those who were once Israelites after the flesh but are now the Israel of God or the spiritual children of Abraham.[6] I conclude this discussion with the splendid statement of Wilkinson: "We believe there is not one single instance in the Word of God, Old Testament or New, in which the term Israel can legitimately be applied to any but the natural descendants of Jacob."[7]

There are certain necessary distinctions to be made between Israel and the Church which, when made, are not only beneficial to believers but to Israel as well. For instance, how consistent can a believer be in his thinking on the Word, and how effectively can he take the Gospel to the Jew, when he literalizes all the Scriptures on the first advent of the Messiah, but spiritualizes all those having references to the second advent of the Messiah and His earthly kingdom so that they are ful-

---

[4] C. Gore, *The Epistle to the Romans* (London: Murray, 1920), 2:35.

[5] W. Sanday and A. C. Headlam, *A Critical and Exegetical Commentary on the Epistle to the Romans*, 5th ed. (Edinburgh: T. & T. Clark, 1977), p. 229.

[6] C. J. Ellicott, *St. Paul's Epistle to the Galatians* (London: Longman's Green, Reader-Dyer, 1867), p. 143.

[7] J. Wilkinson, *Israel My Glory* (London: Mildmay Mission, 1921), p. 21.

filled in the Church? This is an intermingling that has wrought great havoc to the Church. Someone has well said: "The spiritualizing of Israel's blessings has meant the carnalizing of the Church." The only remedy for such confusion is to draw for ourselves clear distinctions between Israel and the Church.

In his work on ecclesiology Dr. Chafer has well pointed out some two dozen contrasts between Israel and the Church.[8] I note only those which are the more striking. In Genesis 22:17 God had promised Abraham a seed as the stars of the heaven and as the sand that is upon the seashore, speaking of an earthly and a heavenly seed. Israel's promises, hopes, and blessings are all earthly; those of the Church are heavenly.

This is well illustrated by the book of Joshua and the epistle to the Ephesians. In the first, the goal is possession of the land of Palestine with all the blessings attendant upon such an occupation in obedience to God. In the second, the sphere is heavenly, the warfare is heavenly, and the blessings are all spiritual in Christ Jesus in the heavenlies. Failure to discern God's earthly and heavenly purposes has been the cause of much of false Bible teaching.

The consummation of God's purposes for Israel will be realized when Israel, as a converted nation, will dwell in the land of Palestine under the rule of the Son of David on the Davidic throne in Jerusalem, with blessings flowing out to all the nations of the earth. God's purpose in the Church is that through the substitutionary death of the Lord Jesus Christ, He might show the exceeding riches of His grace in His kindness toward us through Christ Jesus. Are not these purposes wholly divergent from one another? The only point of contact between them is that they are both dependent upon the Lord Jesus Christ for their complete and final fulfillment.

All is contrast between Israel and the Church as far as nationality is concerned. In my above definition of Israel I have shown that this nation is composed of all the natural

---

[8] L. S. Chafer, *Systematic Theology* (Dallas: Dallas Sem., 1947), 4:47-53.

descendants of Abraham through Jacob. It is a physical birth
which entitles the individual to his standing in the nation.
With the Church, however, the situation is decidedly otherwise. In the first place, she is composed of members from all
the nations upon the face of the earth. In the second place,
the individual is entitled to his position by virtue of a spiritual
or new birth. Need there be confusion here when the Scriptures are so clear and explicit in these particulars?

The Church and Israel did not come into existence at the
same time nor are they coterminous upon the earth. Israel
had its beginning from the call of Abram from Ur of the
Chaldees and will be found on earth in all ages. The Church,
however, had its inception at Pentecost when the Holy Spirit
came to abide with believers after having baptized them into
the Body of Christ. Her pilgrimage on earth will be termi-
nated by the rapture. The distinction is clear: Israel is in all
dispensations from that of the promise, while the Church is in
the dispensation of grace only.

Israel was governed (and will be in the millennial age) by a
principle wholly foreign to that which is in force in the
Church age. Israel was under the Mosaic system which expected one to "Do and live" and "Do and be." It afforded no
divine enablement, but could only pronounce finally:
"Cursed be he that confirmeth not all the words of this law to
do them." It was a system based upon works and dependent
upon the energy of the flesh for its execution. The principle
governing the Church is that of grace. It is based upon promises in grace and looks to God for its fulfillment. It expects
one to "Live and do" and "Be and do." First the individual is
constituted a son of God, then he is asked to do with the
enablement of the Holy Spirit those things which are worthy
of the vocation wherewith he is called. The apostle Paul
through the Spirit definitely states what things are required of
the believer. They are as high above the Law requirements as
heaven is above the earth.

Paul reveals that believers are to reckon themselves dead
indeed to sin, but alive unto God through Jesus Christ our

Lord. They are to yield themselves unto God as those that are
alive from the dead, and their members as instruments of
righteousness to God. They are to cleanse themselves from all
filthiness of the flesh and spirit, perfecting holiness in the fear
of God. They are to walk in the Spirit and not fulfill the lusts
of the flesh.They are through the Spirit to mortify the deeds
of the body and to live. They are to recognize that they who
are Christ's have crucified the flesh with the affections and
lusts. They are to put off concerning the former conversation
the old man, which is corrupt according to the deceitful lusts,
and being renewed in the spirit of their minds, to put on the
new man, which after God is created in righteousness and
true holiness.

Paul reveals that believers are to live soberly, righteously,
and godly in this present world, looking for that blessed hope
and the glorious appearing of the great God and our Saviour
Jesus Christ. Less than these requirements could not be asked
of those who have been constituted sons of God, citizens of
heaven, those seated in the heavenlies with Christ. In its requirements the Law commands; grace exhorts. Failure to
comply with the enactments of the Law brings punishment; in
grace failure robs of peace and abounding joy, and stunts
spiritual growth. Is it possible to find two such groups as
Israel and the Church whose governing principles differ so
decidedly in their essential characteristics, yet are so often
confused? I could multiply contradistinctions such as these,
but I feel that those indicated above will suffice for our present purpose.

It remains for me to define what I mean by "blindness." It
goes without saying that this is not a physical loss of sight.
The word used in Romans 11:25 is *porosis* which, as Sanday
and Headlam point out, comes from the verb *poroo*, a medi-
cal term used in Hippocrates and elsewhere to denote a hard
substance growing when bones are fractured.[9] In Scripture
this is used to denote the covering that grows over the heart,

---

[9] Sanday and Headlam, *Romans*, p. 314.

as an outcome of repeated disobedience, which renders men unapproachable with the truth and causes them to be insensible to the wrong they are doing. This *porosis* or hardening is strictly a matter of the heart, which is the center of all spiritual life, "the fountain and seat of the thoughts, passions, desires, appetites, affections, purposes and endeavors."[10]

Before closing this introduction it may be well to indicate the purpose and plan of this study. Being convinced from the Scriptures that the history of Israel is an integral unit, I expect to treat it as such. In this way the restricted field or scope of the mystery itself will gain prominence. Against the background of all Israel's history, I believe, can the mystery of Israel's blindness best be seen in its proper perspective. I shall follow in the main (and only so) Paul's division of his great theodicy in Romans 9, 10, and 11: Israel's past, present, and future.

Israel's Past: Elected

Anyone who reads the book of Genesis with any degree of insight at all cannot fail to be impressed with the seeming disproportionate division of the book. In the first eleven chapters of the book are the account of creation, the temptation, the entrance of sin and death into the world, the flood, the dissemination of the nations over the whole earth, and the multiplication of their languages. The remainder of the book is occupied principally and primarily with the history of one man's family, that of Abraham. How disproportionate the book is! Not so, for there is a purpose behind it all. Through Abraham God had purposed to reclaim the fallen race to Himself and shower His grace on all who would be willing to receive it. God chose Abraham as the medium, and it is to this principle of choice, election, that I now turn.

---

[10] J. H. Thayer, *A Greek-English Lexicon of the New Testament* (Grand Rapids: Zondervan, 1956), p. 325.

The fact of this election is enunciated throughout the Word of God. Moses, in rehearsing the gracious dealings of God with the nation Israel, declares that because God loved Abraham, Isaac, and Jacob, He chose their seed after them and brought them out of Egypt, driving out greater and mightier nations than Israel, in order that they might possess the land (Deuteronomy 4:37-38). In Deuteronomy 7:6-8 Moses affirms that the Lord God had chosen Israel to be a special people unto Himself above all the nations of the earth, not because they were greater in number; they were the fewest of all people. Nor was it for their righteousness or the uprightness of their heart. The choice was solely because God loved them. The psalmist is setting forth the same truth when he praises God that He has chosen Jacob unto Himself and Israel for His peculiar treasure (Psalm 135:4). The prophet Isaiah, likewise, proclaims that Israel was God's servant, chosen sovereignly by Him (Isaiah 41:8-9). Finally, the apostle Paul concludes his message on Israel in Romans 11:28 by stating that Israel were enemies of the Gospel for the Gentiles' sakes, but as concerning the election they were beloved for the fathers' sakes (see also Exodus 33:13, 16; Deuteronomy 9:4-6; 32:8-9; 2 Samuel 7:23-24; Isaiah 43:21).

Because Romans 9 is the central passage in the Bible on election, it is well to look into the subject. Furthermore, the question as to the character of Israel's election gains importance when one considers that if Israel were elected as a nation to salvation and then were rejected, we as believers in Christ have no better guarantee that God's choice will remain steadfast in our case. Godet frankly admits that God's rejection of Israel is the enigma of history because it involves the rejection of an election which from the very nature of the case is impossible.

The situation can best be made clear by considering the kinds of election. First of all, there is an election of individuals. This is God's sovereign choice of those who are to be the objects of His salvation. Paul writes the Ephesians that they have been chosen in Christ before the foundation of the world that they should be holy and without blame before Him; in commending the Thessalonians he mentions the fact that he knows their election of God; in saluting Titus he declares that he is an apostle of Jesus Christ according to the faith of God's elect. Peter, in writing to the strangers scattered throughout Pontus, Galatia, Cappadocia, Asia, and Bithynia, designates them as those who are elect according to the foreknowledge of God the Father, through sanctification of the Spirit, unto obedience and sprinkling of the blood of Jesus Christ. Surely this is an election to salvation, eternal life in Jesus Christ. It is wholly an individual matter.

Besides individual election the Scriptures teach a national election. Such was the choice of Israel. It was an election to outward privilege. The choice of Israel was within the sphere of time and had to do with temporal things. In such an election the wicked largely partake of the temporal blessings of the upright, and the righteous share in the judgments of the wicked.[11] A case in point is the sin of Achan. Because of his sin many of the children of Israel fell in the battle at Ai. This national election of Israel is similar to that of individual election only in the fact that they are both unconditional. Wilkinson puts it succinctly when he says: "The national election did not secure eternal salvation for one individual."[12]

The question now before us is: Does Paul speak in Romans 9 of an individual or a national election, and if a national election, is it to privileges or is Paul thinking of them individually as elected to eternal salvation? For with Israel we must distinguish between what is national and that which is individual. Otherwise, if there is only a national election possible to Israel and they have been rejected from that, then there is no more hope for the individual Israelite to be elected to eternal salvation. From a study of the Scriptures I am bound to conclude, however, that it is possible to have an election of individuals to salvation from Israel at the same

---

[11] Wilkinson, *Israel My Glory*, p. 3.
[12] Ibid., p. 45.

time that there is a national election to privilege. With Israel is found an individual election within a national election. This is only true of Israel because she is the only nation in Scripture that has ever been nationally elected.

In commenting on the election in Romans 9, Sanday and Headlam maintain that the argument in the main is applicable to nations and people, but they feel that such phrases as "fitted unto destruction" and "prepared unto glory" cannot be limited to an earthly destiny.[13] Stifler thinks that in God's choice of Israel, "He elected it as a whole to obtain the salvation in Christ when the appointed time for the blessings shall come."[14] Bishop Moule feels that an election to privilege will not adequately explain Paul's use of "election" throughout these chapters in Romans.[15]

This is true, for Paul does speak of an individual election in chapter 11. But what kind of election is there in Romans 9? I feel with Gore, Ironside, Chafer, and Griffith Thomas, that Paul is speaking here of an election to privilege. The implications, then, must be evident. If Israel as a nation was elected to privileges only, then in spite of God's temporary rejection of the nation, it is eminently possible for individuals to be elected of God to eternal salvation at the same time.

Let us now consider the nature of these privileges and the purpose of their bestowal. Paul catalogs the specific privileges of the nation Israel in Romans 9 before he ever draws his distinction between those in Israel who were not only nationally elect but individually chosen as well. The first privilege is the adoption, the *huiothesia*, or the son-placing. This adoption must not be confused with that which is found in the New Testament. In connection with Israel, it was a divine act which constituted the nation as a whole the son of God. Adoption in the New Testament refers to the reception of the believer in Christ at the time of regeneration into the

---

[13] Ibid., p. 347.

[14] James M. Stifler, *The Epistle to the Romans* (Chicago: Moody Press, 1960), p. 184.

[15] H. C. G. Moule, *Studies in Romans* (Grand Rapids: Kregel, 1977), p. 187.

family and household of God. The believer receives the Spirit of adoption whereby he can call God, "Abba, Father."

What adoption meant in the case of Israel can be ascertained from the Scriptures which embody this truth. We first meet with the subject of adoption in Exodus 4:22 where Moses is commanded to say to Pharaoh: *"Thus says the* LORD, *'Israel is My son, My firstborn.'"* Moses reiterates this truth when he reminds Israel in Deuteronomy 14:1: *"You are the sons of the* LORD *your God."* The prophet Hosea, after rebuking Israel for being an empty vine that brings forth fruit only to itself, recalls: *"When Israel was a youth I loved him, and out of Egypt I called My son"* (11:1). Of course, this Scripture has its complete fulfillment in Christ, but no one can reasonably deny its primary application to Israel here. It was indeed a privilege to be called the son of God.

Another privilege was the glory. The glory referred to here is not that glory that was to be done away, spoken of by Paul in 2 Corinthians 3. The glory there is connected with the Law, the ministration of condemnation. The glory here is the Shekinah which dwelt between the cherubim on the Ark of the Covenant. God promised Israel that He would meet with them and the tabernacle would be sanctified by His glory. After Moses had built the tabernacle according to the specifications of the Lord, a cloud covered the tent of the congregation, and the glory of the Lord filled the tabernacle. After Solomon had finished the Temple, the glory of the Lord so filled the house that the priests were not able to stand to minister. This glory in the sanctuary denoted the actual presence of God in their midst to guide and bless.

Yet another privilege was the covenants. All the covenants beginning with Abraham—the Abrahamic, Mosaic, Palestinian, Davidic, and New—were made with Israel. The first was wholly unconditional and one of promise. It is the all-embracing covenant, for according to it all the families of the earth are to be blessed in Abraham's seed, which is Christ. The Mosaic was a conditional covenant and hence was broken. The Palestinian made possession and occupancy of the land, the right of ownership to which was included in the Abrahamic covenant, contingent upon obedience to God while in the land. For this reason Israel can now still have right of title to Palestine and yet not occupy it. It was a conditional covenant and was broken by Israel.

The Davidic covenant assured Israel that of the seed of David they would have a King to reign in Jerusalem during the millennial age. It was an unconditional covenant proceeding from God's tender love for David, a man after His own heart. The New was also an unconditional covenant, but it has never been received by Israel as a nation. This covenant assures redemption from sin through the Saviour Christ Jesus. All the unconditional covenants are still in force, because they are dependent upon God for their fulfillment; all the conditional covenants have been broken by the disobedience of Israel.

A fourth privilege was the giving of the Law. Although many Gentiles erroneously appropriate to themselves the enactments and ordinances of the Law, the Mosaic system was given to Israel only. Moses had asked Israel if they knew of any nation so great that had statutes and judgments so righteous as the Law that God had given them. For we must remember that, although the Law cannot render a man righteous, yet it is itself "holy and just and good" and spiritual, because it partakes of the holy character of God Himself. No small privilege was this giving of the Law to Israel.

The service of God was that characteristic feature of the religious life of Israel which differentiated them most strikingly from all their heathen neighbors. Here was a people which had access to the presence of God through a divinely instituted priesthood, as well as atonement for all sins committed, through a marvelously arranged system of substitutionary sacrifices. How replete with types of the great sacrifice was this service of God! How loudly it testified to all the nations that Israel's God was not only the true and living God, but the holy God as well!

To Israel pertain also the promises. The *epangeliai* here refer primarily to the promises through the Messiah. We believe, however, that all God's gracious promises to Israel in the Old Testament can be included. All these promises can be summed up under five heads: an eternal national entity, an eternal land, an eternal King, an eternal kingdom, and an eternal throne.[16] The prophet Jeremiah, in speaking of the New Covenant to be made with the house of Israel and the house of Judah, declares that the LORD has said that, if the sun shall cease to give light by day and the moon and stars by night, and if heaven above can be measured and the foundations of the earth searched out below, then will He cast off the seed of Israel, so that they shall cease from being a nation before Him forever (Jeremiah 31:35-37). With such an explicit and unequivocal promise Israel need never fear for her national existence. To Abraham God had said: *"For all the land which you see, I will give it to you and to your descendants forever"* (Genesis 13:15). Palestine may not be occupied by the nation Israel as their own land, but the right and title to it have irrevocably been given to them by God.

Concerning Israel's eternal King, Jeremiah is again clear in affirming that if God's covenant of the day and that of the night can be broken, then can His covenant also be broken which promised to David that he should never lack for a son to reign upon his throne (Jeremiah 33:21). Although the heathen may rage and the kings of the earth take counsel together against the Lord and His Christ, yet it is well to bear in mind that God in His eternal purposes which He purposed in Christ Jesus has set His King upon the holy hill of Zion. He has purposed and it shall stand! Who shall hinder Him?

As for Israel's eternal kingdom, the prophets are replete with these promises. To Daniel it was revealed that to the Son of Man that came to the "Ancient of days" (Daniel 7:22), there would be given dominion, glory, and a kingdom, His dominion being an everlasting one and His kingdom, *"one*

---

[16] Chafer, *Systematic Theology*, 4:315-25.

which will not be destroyed" (7:14). God had promised
David, finally, that his throne would exist forever. The psalm
by Ethan the Ezrahite states God's oath to David: *"His
descendants shall endure forever, and his throne as the sun
before Me"* (Psalm 89:36). A nation with such blessed promises as these could well glory in the Lord.

But Paul has not yet recounted all of Israel's privileges. He
gives the greatest last. Israel was favored with being the
nation from which the Messiah came. The promise of the
Redeemer had first been given to Eve, then had come down
through the line of Shem. God might just as easily have
chosen Japheth, but He chose Shem then Abraham. To consider that the Almighty God had chosen them as a nation to
bring forth His Son in whom all of God's purposes are
centered and in whom all nations of the earth are yet to be
blessed, should have been sufficient cause to excite Israel to
never-ending praise and adoration. A nation so favored of
God is assuredly one well beloved of Him.

I already have indicated that Israel was privileged for a certain purpose. This was a threefold purpose. First, the nation
was chosen to witness to the truth of the unity of God. This
may seem quite an unnecessary calling now, but in the midst
of universal idolatry it was most needful. Israel's great
slogan, the last words on the lips of her faithful martyrs is:
"Hear, O Israel! The LORD *is our God, the* LORD *is one"*
(Deuteronomy 6:4). The prophet Isaiah had declared to Israel
that they were the witnesses of the Lord, His servant whom
He had chosen, to show forth that *"I, even I, am the* LORD*"*
(Isaiah 43:11). Second, Israel was to preserve the Scriptures.
When the apostle Paul asked in Romans 3:1 what advantage
the Jew had, he answered that it was much every way, but
"first of all, that they were entrusted with the oracles of God"
(3:2). How well this task, the transmission of the Scriptures,
was accomplished is a matter of common knowledge and the
subject of the profound admiration and unresolved commendation of all scholars of the Hebrew text of the Old
Testament.

An incident that occurred in Brooklyn, New York, some years ago is most interesting in this connection.[17] A member of the Ahavath Moishe ("Love of Moses") Congregation, upon opening the ark of the scrolls in order to conduct the rites of the Passover service, found to his dismay that one of the holy scrolls had been stolen. It was later found in a vacant lot opposite the synagogue; it had been partly burned. Funeral rites, exactly corresponding to those for human beings, were conducted for the scroll, and it was buried in a pine box after having been wrapped in a prayer shawl. The congregation went into mourning for one week. Such is the love of Israel for the Scriptures. As I sit here and write, I can see in my mind's eye my father as he used to kiss the book of the Law again and again after he had finished reading the particular Sabbath portion. Israel did preserve the Scriptures in their purity.

Third, Israel was chosen to be the channel of the Messiah. The unconditional covenant was vouchsafed to Abraham wherein he was told that in his seed, which is Christ, were all the nations of the earth to be blessed. The promise of the seed passed from Abraham to Isaac and then to Jacob. Of the sons of Jacob, Judah was chosen of whom Shiloh would come.

The psalmist David was next favored with word of the Lord that of his loins would come forth He who would reign in righteousness on the Davidic throne in Jerusalem. It remained now for Isaiah only to declare more fully the fact of the virgin birth (implied in the protevangelium of Genesis 3:15). The fulfillment of all these promises concerning the seed is seen in the first verse of Matthew's Gospel: *"The book of the genealogy of Jesus Christ, the son of David, the son of Abraham."* The line had been kept pure in spite of the attempts of Satan to destroy the seed. A greater calling than this, to bring forth Him who is verily God manifest in the flesh, is inconceivable. But all these privileges to the contrary

---

[17] *The Chosen People,* May 1932, p. 13.

notwithstanding, Israel was headed for failure, because "they perverted agency into a monopoly of Divine favour."[18]

When we begin studying the New Testament, it is not long before we see a state of affairs quite different from that obtaining in the Old Testament dispensations. For instance, we hear Paul saying in Romans 3:9 (KJV), *"We have before proved both Jews and Gentiles, that they are all under sin."* Surely Paul could not be putting Israel, as privileged as she was, on the same level as the Gentiles who were aliens from the commonwealth of Israel, strangers from the covenants of promise, having no hope, and without God in the world!

But that is precisely what Paul has done, and this declares most unequivocally that Israel has been rejected from her position of privilege during this present Age of Grace. It is to a study of this parenthetical period that we now turn our attention.

The Scattering of the Nation

In Daniel 9 we read that after the prophet had studied God's Word concerning the end of the desolations of Jerusalem and after he had earnestly poured out his heart before God in true confession of his sins and those of his people, that God sent Gabriel to give him understanding in the matter:

> *"Seventy weeks are determined upon thy people and thy holy city, to finish the transgression, and to make an end of sins, and to make reconciliation for iniquity, and to bring in everlasting righteousness, and to seal up the vision and prophecy, and to anoint the most Holy. Know therefore and understand, that from the going forth of the commandment to restore*

---

[18] Robert Anderson, *The Silence of God* (Grand Rapids: Kregel, 1978), p. 53.

*and to build Jerusalem unto the Messiah the Prince
shall be seven weeks, and threescore and two weeks:
the street shall be built again, and the wall, even in
troublous times. And after threescore and two weeks
shall Messiah be cut off, but not for himself: and the
people of the prince that shall come shall destroy the
city and the sanctuary; and the end thereof shall be
with a flood, and unto the end of the war desolations
are determined. And he shall confirm the covenant
with many for one week: and in the midst of the week
he shall cause the sacrifice and the oblation to cease,
and for the overspreading of abominations he shall
make it desolate, even until the consummation, and
that determined shall be poured upon the desolate."*
(Daniel 9:24-27, KJV)

Needless to say, this is one of the most interesting prophecies of the Word. We shall not attempt a detailed study of this wonderful prophecy; we will make several observations. It is evident that the prophecy concerns Israel, for Gabriel speaks of "thy people," Daniel's people. Furthermore, the weeks spoken of *(shabhuim)* are not meant to be seven-day weeks. They are rather heptads of years or 490 years. (This is substantiated by Daniel 10:2 where "three full weeks" is a translation of *sheloshah shabhuim yamim* or "three weeks of days." In this case, the weeks are seven-day weeks.) The division of these weeks is as follows: (1) seven weeks or forty-nine years, (2) sixty-two weeks or 434 years, (3) one week or seven years. The beginning of this reckoning is to be the time of the decree to restore and build Jerusalem, which was in the twentieth year of Artaxerxes or 445 B.C. (Nehemiah 2).[19]

From that time till Messiah the Prince there were to be sixty-nine weeks or 483 years, and it is only another proof of the infallibility of the Word of our God that the Lord Jesus

---

[19] A. C. Gaebelein, *The Prophet Daniel* (Grand Rapids: Kregel, 1968), pp. 130-40.

Christ entered Jerusalem (according to the reckoning of the prophetic years) at the expiration of the sixty-ninth week. Then we have the prophecy of the death of the Messiah and the destruction of Jerusalem.

There remains now but one week of the prophecy, and from the nature of its prediction it is readily seen that it has not been fulfilled. The clock of God stopped at the end of the sixty-ninth week and the Jewish age has been interrupted. This interval is the Church age, not foreseen in the Old Testament. It is this interval that solves the problem that troubled the prophets when they searched for the specific time of the sufferings of Christ and that of the glory that should follow. The Lord Jesus made this clear in the synagogue at Nazareth when He stopped in the midst of Isaiah's prophecy in 61:1-3, and announced what part of it was then being fulfilled.

This interval is further brought into prominence from a study of the gospel according to Matthew. The gospel begins with the Lord's ministry among Israel, His preaching of the Gospel of the Kingdom, His great signs and miracles, and His choosing of the twelve disciples to *"go to the lost sheep of the house of Israel"* (Matthew 10:6). In chapter 11 the Lord upbraids the cities wherein most of His mighty works had been done, and at the end of chapter 12 He breaks all human ties by declaring that whoever did His will would be His brother, sister, and mother. Dispensationally considered, Matthew 13 is most important, for in it the Lord foretells of the previously unforeseen period known as the age of Christendom, wherein good and evil coexist until the end.

When we study the interval in Daniel 9 and that predicted in Matthew 13, we become convinced that it is the same period of which Paul is speaking in Romans 9:22 through 10:21. He is here demonstrating that God had forewarned Israel that because of her sin—specifically here, that of the crucifixion of Christ—she would be set aside and the Gentiles would come into blessing. Hosea had prophesied that God would call a people His people which were not His people.

Isaiah had foretold that if it were not for the Lord, Israel would have been left as Sodom and Gomorrah.

The rejection of the Lord Jesus Christ and His subsequent crucifixion constituted the greatest calamity of all Israel's history. Those were solemn words for Israel that the Lord uttered when He told them that their house was left desolate unto them and that they would not see Him again till they said: *"'Blessed is He who comes in the name of the Lord'"* (Matthew 23:38-39). This rejection was not caused by Israel's idolatry as had been their exile to Babylon, for Caligula could complain of Israel that in all of Asia there was not one single place that had refused to receive his statue for worship, except in Judea.[20] The rejection of Israel between the two advents of the Messiah, between Daniels' sixty-ninth and seventieth week, is the result of her rejection of Him in whom all her hopes and promises had been centered.

During the time of Israel's rejection she is scattered, persecuted, and blind. The scattering of Israel had been the subject of Moses' prophecy in the Book of Deuteronomy. He foretold: *"The* Lord *shall scatter you among the nations"; "The* Lord *shall scatter thee among all people, from one end of the earth even unto the other"; "I said, I would scatter them into corners"* (Deuteronomy 4:27; 28:64; 32:26, KJV). Before His crucifixion Christ, predicting the destruction of Jerusalem, said of Israel that *"they shall fall by the edge of the sword, and shall be led away captive into all nations"* (Luke 21:24, KJV). Blessing for Israel has been linked with dwelling in the land. How literally the words of Christ and the prophets have been fulfilled in this instance! The Jew has been the man without a country, the wandering Jew. They are to be found in every country of the world. There are white Jews and black Jews, Indian Jews, French Jews, German Jews, English Jews, American Jews, and so on. But always they are Jews, for God in His scattering of them has preserved their national existence for His yet future purposes.

---

[20] A. Saphir, *Book of Hebrews* (New York: Gospel Publ., 1902).

Israel scattered has not meant Israel blessed. Far from it, for she has been hounded and persecuted to this day. To read the tale of Israel's woes is to learn of a people which has been the object of the hatred of all nations. But so it is always: the world always hates that which God has loved. Israel's woes began, as Christ had predicted, with the destruction of Jerusalem. Josephus relates: "It appears that the misfortunes of all men from the beginning of the world, if compared to these of the Jews, are not so considerable." After the scattering of the Jews from Palestine they dwelt in various countries with comparative safety.[21]

The Nation's Night of Terror

Her night of terror began with the Crusades. The motivating cause, the course, and the results of the Crusades are well known to every high school boy and girl, but few know the sufferings which the Jews underwent during this time. The Jews in Germany bore the brunt of the persecutions. Before the Crusades they had dwelt in Germany in peace and had possessions of land. Religious freedom also was allowed them. The first ranks of the Crusaders plundered Jew and Christian alike. But when the French and English followed, the time for the murdering of the Jews had begun. One monk after another incited the mobs against the Jews by all sorts of promises of future blessedness and by lies to the effect that an inscription on the grave of Jesus had declared that the compulsory conversion of the Jews was the duty of all true believers.

In city after city the Jewish inhabitants were left to decide between the sword and baptism. Such was the terror aroused in the hearts of the Jews that when they heard of the approach of the Crusaders, parents killed their own children; women and girls, loading themselves with stones, threw themselves into rivers. Those that survived were brutally slaughtered by the bloodthirsty armies after witnessing the destruction of their homes, the plundering of their goods, and the burning of the Scriptures.

In the great city of Worms many of the Jews had gained the protection of Bishop Allebrandus. It was not long, however, before the Crusaders made a raid on the bishop's palace, it appears, and demanded that the Jews be turned over to them. The bishop then informed the Jews that they would have to be baptized in order to enjoy his further protection. The Jews asked for time to consider. When the time had elapsed and the bishop went to receive the answer, he found some of them dead in their own blood. When the infuriated mob heard this, they murdered the survivors and dragged their corpses through the streets.

After the massacre at Worms the Crusaders moved on to the city of Mayence. Here the unscrupulous Archbishop Ruthard had craftily invited the Jews to take shelter in his palace. When their surrender was demanded, the mob was allowed to seize them without any opposition on the part of the archbishop's guard. The horrible massacre at Worms was then reenacted.

How true were the words of Moses when he warned Israel that they would become "an astonishment, a proverb, and a byword, among all nations!" Many a time did they cry in the morning: "Would God it were even!" And in the evening they said: "Would God it were morning!" Wrath was truly come upon them to the uttermost.

But the worst was yet to befall them. They were to be driven from place to place. In England, the accession of Edward I brought to the Jews some feeling of security, because they looked upon the king as a just monarch. The king showed them no favors, but neither did he extort their wealth from them. He protected their persons and their property. All was indeed going well until a Dominican monk, in studying the Hebrew language in order to be able to convert the Jews, became converted to Judaism, even undergoing the rite of circumcision. The monk was handed over to the Archbishop of

Canterbury for punishment, but from all appearances he escaped without injury.

The Dominicans, smarting under the disgrace that this member of the order had brought upon them, resolved to take vengeance on the Jews. The order first sought the ear of the queen, who shortly afterward expelled the Jews from the town of Cambridge which was her property, and aroused ill feeling toward the Jews among the merchants of the whole country. Soon Parliament began to pass discriminating laws against the Jews. The Jews were compelled to wear a distinguishing badge that pointed them out as Jews. Every opportunity that afforded itself of draining them of their wealth was seized upon.

Shortly after this a charge of counterfeiting the coin of the realm was brought against them, for which many were hanged, others sentenced to life imprisonment, and yet others were expelled from the country while their property was confiscated. The next accusation brought against them was that the Jews of Northampton had crucified a Christian child. The outcome of this was that many Jews in London were torn asunder by horses and their dead bodies were hanged on the gallows. It was not long before other accusations were forthcoming and similar penalties inflicted. Finally, in 1290, the king, through the influence of others, issued a decree that all the Jews of England were to be expelled from the country. Failure to leave the country was to be punished by hanging. From England many Jews went to France.

The misfortune of the Jews in France began in the last quarter of the twelfth century. During the reign of Louis VII they lived in safety and were protected from the attacks of the clergy. Louis paid little heed to the resolutions of the Lateran Council, and he was most lenient in the enforcement of papal decisions. When his son, Philip Augustus, came to the throne, matters changed for the worse. Since Philip was not a great landowner, and land meant power in those days, he concocted means whereby he might acquire money to further his interests. He immediately called the Jews to account for their usury and compelled them to pay him huge sums for their exoneration from the accusation brought against them that they slaughtered Christian children so that they might have their blood for the feast of Passover. He had them cast wholesale into prison and made them buy their freedom with large payments of money. Misery upon misery followed them until in 1181 the king issued an edict forcing all the Jews to leave his province. Upon their departure the king enriched himself with their property. Since the estate of the king was not very large, the Jews settled in other parts of France.

What Philip Augustus had begun, Louis IX carried on. He soon exiled the Jews from his territory, but a few years later they were permitted the right to return. A year before his death he ordered the wearing of a badge of red felt or saffron yellow cloth in the form of a disc upon the breast and back of every Jew. This was done so that they might be recognized from all sides. In the middle of the fourteenth century during the time of the great epidemic known as the Black Death, it was from the southern portion of France that the rumor originated that the Jews had poisoned the brooks and the wells. In one town a whole Jewish congregation of men, women, and children was burned to death with the Scriptures by the incited populace.

There is no need to multiply details, for in our own century we know of the trial of Captain Dreyfus. It was at this trial, where Dr. Theodore Herzl as a reporter saw the deep-seated hatred of some of the French people for the Jews, that political Zionism was born in his heart.

Looking at the history of the Jews in Poland, we find no better situation. During the last half of the sixteenth century Poland was a place of refuge for the Jews where they could live unmolested lives and develop their interests without compulsion or restraint. When persecuted in other countries the Jews found a haven of shelter in Poland. The Talmudic schools and seminaries that grew up then have been the source of much of the Talmudic teaching here in America today. But this respite was not to be for long, for the Catholic clergy viewed their development and interests with hatred and envy.

Matters went from bad to worse when the Polish kings invited the Jesuit monks to train the young nobles and the clergy. The Jews soon began to feel oppression in their trades. It was not long afterward that the kings, to gain the aid of the Cossacks in warding off the invasion of the Tartars, gave the former some independence in the Ukraine and Little Russia. The Jews were indeed blind when they offered their aid to the ambitious nobility and the Jesuits in suppressing the Cossacks. When the Cossacks came into the ascendancy, they wreaked vengeance upon the Jews. Plunder, murder, destruction of homes and synagogues, and heartless massacre were the order of the day. There was such a large number of fugitive Jews at the time of their expulsion from Poland, that the German communities to which they fled were obliged to use in their maintenance the money intended for the poor Jews of Jerusalem who were being drained at the time by the pasha and his followers.

The tale of Israel's woe reaches its climax with the persecutions in Spain. Nowhere in Europe had the Jews enjoyed greater freedom of belief than in Spain. The learning of the Spanish Talmudical schools was almost proverbial. Many have spoken of the tenth century in Spain as the golden age of Jewish science, literature, philosophy, and learning. Jews were held in high esteem and occupied high offices in the land. It is to the Jews of Spain that the Western world is indebted for the transmission of much Arabian science, philosophy, and learning. The first persecution, though purely local, that the Jews suffered was in Granada. It lasted for some time and many were compelled to sell their property and to leave.

There was another persecution of the Jews (eleventh century) in Andalusia by Muslims from Granada, but it was not prolonged. The storm clouds began to gather with the establishment by Pope Gregory IX of the Inquisition to root out heresy, especially that of the Albigenses. It was this holy Inquisition that caused a Jewish poet to call Spain "the hell of the Jews." Nowhere did they suffer as in Spain. The most intense persecutions were during the reign of Ferdinand of Aragon and Isabella of Castile. Their "holy zeal" seemingly knew no bounds. Every inhabitant of the land was called upon by those of the inquisitorial office to become an informer of all those guilty of Jewish heresy. The Jewish heresy was really all the tenets of the Jewish faith.

At the outset several thousand Jews were cast into prison. The *auto-da-fe* was instituted in 1481. It consisted of the public torment of all heretics before they were thrown to the flames. Nor were the officials satisfied with the persecution of the living, for they unearthed the corpses of proselytes who had died in heresy, burnt them, confiscated the possessions of their heirs, and reduced them to abject poverty. So terrible were the persecutions that many Jews (called *Marranos*, a derisive term meaning "swine") feigned belief in Christianity and were baptized. In this century such a group petitioned the chief rabbi of Jerusalem for reinstatement into the Jewish religion. It was not long before the Inquisition of heresy had spread its talons over the whole of Spain. An unrelenting Dominican monk, Torquemada, was made inquisitor-general of Spain. A mark of infamy, composed of flaming crosses upon their clothing, was imposed upon the Jews. A Jew of that time wrote:

> In these days the smoke of the martyr's pyre rises unceasingly to heaven in all the Spanish kingdoms and the isles. One-third of the Marranos have perished in the flames, another third wander homeless over the earth seeking where they may hide themselves, and the remainder live in perpetual terror of a trial.[22]

After the conquest of Granada, Ferdinand and Isabella decreed, in spite of the fact that even the pope did not sup-

---

[22] Ibid., 4:332.

port it, that within four months all Jews were to leave Spain. The Jews exerted their utmost influence and offered great sums of money for the revocation of the edict. The king, intent on enriching himself, was inclined to yield when the infuriated Torquemada rushed into the presence of the king and queen waving a crucifix and saying: "Judas Iscariot sold the Lord for thirty pieces of silver; you wish to sell him now for 300,000 ducats!" The impression was inevitable and the doom of the Jews was sealed. At the appointed time the Jews left Spain in 1492, many dying along the way of starvation and privations.

I have before me the December 1931 copy of *The Chosen People* which indicates that Senator Fulida of the New Spanish Republic issued a call for the Jews to return to Spain. These nations that have persecuted Israel have yet to learn that God was (I say it reverently) in earnest when He declared: *"I will bless them that bless thee, and curse him that curseth thee"* (Genesis 12:3, KJV). Israel is still the apple of His eye, beloved for the fathers' sake.

From Spain many Jews went to Turkey, Russia, and to other Eastern countries to seek a place of refuge. Russia had shown her attitude toward the Jews in the Cossack Wars when she joined arms with the Cossacks against the Jews. The story of Russian persecution brings us to comparatively recent times. Their lot had been bearable under the Emperor Alexander I who had tried to improve their condition. But the privileges granted at the time were shortly afterward nullified when those who dwelt in the country were ordered to move into the cities within a specified amount of time. Needless to say, this hindered the development of the Jewish communities.

Under the Soviet regime the Jews are now drinking the cup of sorrow to the dregs. Reports of recent years have been to the effect that officials are torturing whole Jewish communities in order to extort money. Those who do not have money are compelled to write to their relatives in America to ask for money. Tens of thousands of Jews are being tortured in an unspeakable manner. Letters have been addressed from Palestine to leading Jews in America confirming the report.[23] Later reports continue to tell of the sad condition of the Jews in Russia, with brighter prospects unlikely for the future.

Finally, we turn to the condition of the Jews in Germany. We have already referred at the outset of this discussion to the persecutions of the Jews in Germany during the Crusades. For many years the blood accusation—that Jews use the blood of Christian children for the Passover feast—was used to bring about the massacre of the Jews. After the death of Emperor Frederick II, thousands of Jews were slain. In Sinzig all the members of the congregation were burned alive on a Sabbath while they were worshiping in the synagogue. In 1283 the finding of a dead Christian child about Easter time was the occasion for pillaging of the Jewish homes.

The history of the Jews in the first half of the fourteenth century is full of murders, assaults, persecutions, and massacres. They were made to pay all kinds of ridiculous taxes and were subject to every type of indignity. Whenever those who were debtors to the Jews wished to throw off this burden, they found it best accomplished by arousing the populace by some such lie as that a Jew had been seen desecrating the host by piercing it with a knife until blood flowed from it. At the appointed time, then, the mob fell upon the defenseless Jews, killed them, and subsequently confiscated their property, which act had been the purpose of the accusation.

Needless to say, the state of the Jews in Germany became far worse with the persecutions initiated by Adolf Hitler. No one can fully tell the whole tale of sorrow that was enacted in that country, as well as throughout the continent of Europe. The Jewish population of the world before World War II was about 16,500,000. Nearly six million Jews were slaughtered by the Nazis and their allies. In Germany in 1938 within a few days almost 600 synagogues were destroyed. The decree of July 6, 1939, determined to speed up Jewish emigration and

---

[23] *The Chosen People*, March 1932, pp. 10-11.

"get the last Jew out of the Reich." In the Buchenwald concentration camp the death rate was 30 percent of the inmates. Similar conditions obtained in Sachsenhausen and Dachau. After liberation what was found in the concentration camps caused one American correspondent to say: "If I had not seen it, I could not have believed it." The sad story can be summarized somewhat by the following figures: there were 525,000 Jews in Germany; 224,000 in May, 1939; and only 8,000 Jews by 1945.[24]

And for Israel the end is not yet. The Lord Jesus Christ with breaking heart fully foresaw this long night for Israel when He stretched out His arms to receive them as a hen does her chickens, but they would not. O Jerusalem, Jerusalem, how long will you turn from the light and life and love of Him who seeks only your blessedness and peace?

Tracing the Nation's Hardness of Heart

Israel has been not only scattered and persecuted during this Church age, but she has been judicially blinded as well. What the blindness of Israel really means and what the implications of this hardening may be, are subjects not very well understood by the majority of Christians. How this whole subject correlates itself with the program of the Gospel of God's grace in regard to Israel is even less understood. I preface my remarks by stating that it is a mistake to believe that the judicial blindness of Israel now is due to the rejection of Christ over 1,900 years ago by their forefathers, thus rendering their conversion today an impossibility.[25]

Dr. Gaebelein has touched the crux of the matter:

The judicial blindness is certainly not to be understood that every Jew is born with this blindness upon

---

[24] For fuller details, see *Jewish Year Book* (London) for 1940-50 and *American Jewish Year Book* (Philadelphia: Jewish Pub. Soc. of Amer.) for 1939-40, 1940-41, and 1945-46. Incidents of anti-Semitism up through 1973 may be followed in *Britannica Book of the Year, 1973* (New York: Encyclopaedia Britannica), pp. 60, 269, as well as earlier volumes.
[25] Wilkinson, *Israel My Glory*, p. 162.

him. Far be this thought! Every generation of Jews, in refusing the light which shines for all, in sharing the sin of their fathers in rejecting their Messiah, in continuing in their evil ways of unbelief, is put under the sentence of this judicial blindness. The Jew may see if he so chooses and he may refuse the light. God declared in His Word beforehand what would happen to them in this respect.[26]

Let us now turn to a consideration of the progress of Israel's blindness, for it falls historically into several periods. Moses had not led the people of Israel very long before it was evident to him that he was dealing with "a stiffnecked people." At every stage of the journey he was repeatedly confronted with their murmurings and their hardness of heart. More than once did Moses declare: *"The LORD spoke further to me, saying, 'I have seen this people, and indeed, it is a stubborn people'"* (Deuteronomy 9:13). The command came: *"Circumcise then your heart, and stiffen your neck no more"* (10:16). The stiff neck is the inevitable outcome of the hard heart and its ever present accompaniment.

Instead of glorying in the wondrous goodness of the Lord who in His mercy and grace had taken them from their misery and wretchedness, who had gone before them in a pillar of cloud by day and in a pillar of fire by night to lead the way, who had set before them a promised land that flowed with milk and honey, they continually rebelled, set at nought the goodness of God, and limited the Holy One of Israel until Moses in all truth testified to them: *"The LORD hath not given you an heart to perceive, and eyes to see, and ears to hear, unto this day"* (Deuteronomy 29:4, KJV). God is spoken of here as withholding from them spiritual insight and spiritual perception, the very thing against which they had hardened their hearts to receive. The culmination of Israel's disobedi-

---

[26] A. C. Gaebelein, *The Jewish Question* (New York: Our Hope, 1912), p. 33.

ence under Moses came at Kadesh-barnea where God finally made it known that that generation would by no means enter the land; the whole generation, except Caleb and Joshua, was to die in the wilderness.

When Joshua assumed the leadership of the new generation under the command of God, he found that his task was no easier than that of Moses. Comparatively speaking, however, Joshua had less disobedience with which to contend than Moses. The Word bears witness that *"Israel served the* LORD *all the days of Joshua, and all the days of the elders that overlived Joshua"* (Joshua 24:31, KJV). But when we come to the period of the judges we are met with one grand recital of the apostasies of Israel. Each defection from the Lord was more grievous and more sustained than the previous ones. Judges were the means that God used to deliver Israel from the hands of their oppressors. Israel's wanderings from God always made her a prey to her neighbors, but it seemed as though chastisement was the only way for Israel to come back to the Lord. It is safe to say that the period of the Judges is one of the darkest periods in the history of Israel. An age that ended with a situation where *"everyone did what was right in his own eyes,"* could easily be the forerunner of one in which the people desired to throw off the theocracy for an earthly monarchy. And so it was with Israel.

But this hardness of Israel's heart had not yet run its course. The prophetic history of God's people is merely one in which men of God were sent to win Israel from their sin and disobedience. The Jewish people have always prided themselves upon their prophets, but they would do well to consider their shame that the reason for the rise of the prophets lay in the repeated defection of the people from God and the true worship of Himself. When we turn to the prophet Isaiah we see a close connection between his ministry and the fact of Israel's hardness of heart.

After the Lord had given the man of God a glimpse of His sovereign Being, had shown him his own sinfulness, and had cleansed him, He then commissioned him to go to His people. But what an exceedingly strange ministry! He was told:

> *"Go, and tell this people, Hear ye indeed, but understand not; and see ye indeed, but perceive not. Make the heart of this people fat, and make their ears heavy, and shut their eyes; lest they see with their eyes, and hear with their ears, and understand with their heart, and convert, and be healed. Then said I, Lord, how long? And he answered, Until the cities be wasted without inhabitant, and the houses without man, and the land be utterly desolate, and the* LORD *have removed men far away, and there be a great forsaking in the midst of the land. But yet in it shall be a tenth, and it shall return, and shall be eaten: as a teil tree, and as an oak, whose substance is in them, when they cast their leaves: so the holy seed shall be the substance thereof."*   (Isaiah 6:9-13, KJV)

The importance of this Scripture will be more readily realized when we consider that this passage is more often quoted in the New Testament than any other Old Testament text.[27] (See also Matthew 13:14-15; Mark 4:12; Luke 8:10; John 12:40; Acts 28:26.) From this commission it is evident that Isaiah's ministry was to be one of hardening. What is meant is not that God directly and arbitrarily hardens the hearts of men, but that God allows the natural evil impulses of their hearts to go unhindered and unchecked until through their own choices they have become more and more calloused.[28] It is of further interest that in this passage all three figurative expressions for hardening are used: *hishmin,* "to make fat"; *hikhbidh,* "to make heavy"; *heshea,* "to smear over," or "to do to any one what happens to diseased eyes

---

[27] C. Neil, *The Expositor's Commentary on Romans* (London: Dickson, 1882), p. 352.
[28] L. Boettner, *Reformed Doctrine of Predestination* (Phillipsburgh, N.J.: Presbyterian and Reformed), p. 112.

when their sticky secretion during the night becomes a closing crust."[29]

Perception and understanding will be withheld from the people because their hearts are not right toward God. Their last state will, of course, be worse than their first, because the more unceasingly the prophet preaches, the less will they receive the message, so that their hearts will because of their initial corruption, become more and more impenetrable.[30] Little wonder it is, then, that the prophet's heart cried out for his people: "Lord, how long?" Isaiah speaks of this blindness of Israel throughout his prophecy. He asks through the Spirit: *"Who is blind, but my servant? or deaf, as my messenger that I sent? who is blind as he that is perfect, and blind as the* LORD's *servant?"* (42:19, KJV). Nor is Isaiah alone in declaring the blindness of Israel, for Jeremiah, Ezekiel, Daniel, and some of the minor prophets bear similar testimony to the fact that *"'an ox knows its owner, and a donkey its master's manger, but Israel does not know, My people do not understand'"* (Isaiah 1:3).

The hardening of Israel reached its culmination in the ministry and death of the Lord Jesus Christ. The progress of Israel's blindness from the time of the prophets to the time of the rejection of Christ is well illustrated by the parable of the householder who planted a vineyard and let it out to husbandmen before he departed for a far country. When the time of the fruit arrived, the householder sent servants to receive the fruit of the vineyard from the husbandmen. The husbandmen, however, abused the servants, beating one, killing another, and stoning another. When the householder sent other servants, they fared no better than their companions. Finally, the householder sent his son, thinking they would surely reverence him. On the contrary, however, they took him and slew him. The meaning is evident when we remember

---

[29] F. Delitzsch, *Commentary on Isaiah* (Grand Rapids: Eerdmans, 1976), vol. 7, section 1, p. 200.
[30] C. Von Orelli, *The Prophecies of Isaiah* (Edinburgh: T. & T. Clark, 1889), pp. 47, 49.

that God speaks of Israel as His vineyard (Isaiah 5:1-7), and the Lord Jesus had addressed Jerusalem as *"thou that killest the prophets, and stonest them which are sent unto thee"* (Matthew 23:37, KJV).

No prophet of Israel, however, had suffered the indignities that were heaped upon the Lord Jesus Christ. It must be so from the very nature of the case, for He is God manifest in the flesh, very God of very God. When the Lord Jesus first appeared among Israel, Matthew relates that Herod attempted to slay Him. After He had entered upon His public ministry, it was manifest that Israel would have none of Him. They plotted continually how they might destroy Him, and many times they took up stones to stone Him. When the Lord Jesus asked Peter: *"Whom do men say that I the Son of man am?"* (Matthew 16:13, KJV), the reply was to the effect that some thought He was Elijah, that others testified He was Jeremiah, and still others maintained that He was one of the prophets. Strange that no one thought Him to be the Messiah! Note, moreover, the wide difference between the character of a man like Elijah and that of a man like Jeremiah. The only reasonable conclusion is: "They were evidently willing to account for Him by any subterfuge that would relieve them of the acknowledgement of Him as their King."[31] So intent were they on His destruction that two decidedly antagonistic parties such as the Pharisees and the Sadducees could be at one, in plotting His death. When Judas went out to betray the Lord into the hands of His enemies, it was truly night; but it was just as dark a night when the religious leaders of the nation sought to kill Him. They would rather have their "place and nation" than to yield allegiance to Him who came only for blessing.

Since Israel was intent on His rejection, lightly esteeming His person and refusing to receive His testimony and work, the Lord began an altogether different phase of His work,

---

[31] L. S. Chafer, *The Kingdom in History and Prophecy* (New York: Revell, 1915), p. 60.

that in which He is designated as the "Son of Abraham" as well as "Son of David." He began to speak in parables so that the prophecy of Isaiah might have its most complete fulfillment in His ministry. They were to hear His parables but would not understand them because they had already manifested that they loved darkness rather than light.

I believe that the teaching of Christ was then couched in parabolic form to conceal the truth latent therein. In this connection Dr. G. Campbell Morgan contends:

> The purpose of the parable is that of revelation by illustration (we admit that there are illustrative parables that were meant to teach the whole nation originally, such as those in Luke 18:1-14), and the method is always intended to aid and never to hinder understanding. I have made this statement thus of set purpose in order to arrest the attention. I know of nothing more pernicious, than a certain interpretation of the motive which the King had in His use of parables, and I feel that it is of the greatest importance that we should avoid it. I refer to the view that our Lord adopted the parabolic method with His hearers because He had abandoned them in anger, and that His purpose was to hide His truth so that they should not see it. This I most strenuously deny to be true. . . . The parable is an aid, not a hindrance. It veils truth, not that man may not grasp it, but that it shall not escape them.[32]

Dr. Morgan's contention is with the clear, unequivocal, and irrefutable word of Scripture. After the Lord had, therefore, turned from Israel, He directed the hearts of His disciples to the purpose, the salvation of the lost, which had brought Him to earth. Thus He ministered until the hardened

---

[32] G. Campbell Morgan, *The Parables of the Kingdom* (New York: Revell, 1907), p. 16.

hearts of Israel were satisfied with the crucifixion of Him whose last words in their behalf were: "Father, forgive them; for they know not what they do." Such was the calamitous climax of all Israel's blindness and hardening throughout her life's history.

Nor was their condition after Pentecost improved. For, although some believed, the majority rejected the offer of the Holy Spirit's ministry even as they had rejected the loving-kindness of the Father and the undying love of the Son. This hardness of heart continued until Paul could bring the full indictment against them when he declared that they had killed the Lord Jesus and their prophets, they had persecuted the apostles, they did not please God, they were contrary to all men, forbidding the apostles to speak to the Gentiles that they might be saved, for *"the wrath is come upon them to the uttermost"* (1 Thessalonians 2:15-16, KJV).

Choosing False Messiahs

From the time of Christ till this day this hardening of heart has been going on. Especially is this true in regard to the Messiah. The Lord Jesus knew full well whereof He spoke when He said: *"'I have come in My Father's name, and you do not receive Me; if another shall come in his own name, you will receive him"* (John 5:43). I believe the final and complete fulfillment of this prophecy will take place when the nation makes a covenant with the Antichrist, but there have been adumbrations of this truth already. The Jews have received, sometimes in greater and sometimes in lesser numbers, the following false Messiahs: David Alrui, Jacob Frank, Jacob Quorido, Moses Chayim Luzzatto, Mordecai of Eisenstadt, Moses of Crete, Sabbatai Zevi, and others. I choose the last named to give a short account of this imposture.[33].

Sabbatai Zevi (born in 1626 and died in 1676) was a resident of Smyrna in Asia Minor and a contemporary of Spinoza. In his youth Zevi showed signs of an uncontrollable

---

[33] H. Graetz, *History of the Jews*, 5:119-166.

fancy and later engaged with great zest in the study of the Kabbala (lit., "tradition"), the mystic literature of the Jews. He lived an extremely ascetic life. At the age of twenty he had a small circle of followers. His was an attractive personality. The father of Zevi, being a merchant, came into great wealth when he was made the Smyrna agent of an English mercantile house. This success he attributed to his son. It was not long before the father heard discussions in the English house concerning the approaching Millennium in the year 1666. These conversations he communicated to his family, of whom Sabbatai was a most eager listener.

In 1648, the date set by the Kabbala for the inauguration of the age of redemption, Sabbatai Zevi uttered the full name of God, *YHWH*, the Tetragrammaton, which is prohibited by the Talmud and the custom of ages and which was said to be allowed to the high priest only in the Holy of Holies on the Day of Atonement. This Zevi did in the presence of his followers. It was not long before the rabbis banished Zevi and his pupils from Smyrna. About fifteen years later (1666) the rumor broke out again that Zevi in Turkey was the Messiah, this time being supported by one Yachini who claimed possession of an ancient manuscript that undoubtedly declared the Messiahship of Zevi. Then began a series of scenes which Zevi enacted for the benefit of the Kabbalists. On one occasion he prepared a feast, invited his friends, sent for the Law, and declared that he was to celebrate his marriage with it. From Turkey he journeyed to Jerusalem where he hoped to set forth his full claims. I pass over the details of the story relating to his "spiritual" marriage with a Polish-Jewish maiden. Suffice it to say, she attracted many youths to the movement who had no sympathy with the Messianic movement.

Zevi in the meantime was gaining influential and wealthy followers. Because of the intense opposition of the rabbis, Zevi was compelled to leave Jerusalem, but not before he had dispatched messengers to herald his arrival in the Asiatic communities that he intended to visit. Everywhere he was received in triumph. On the day of the Jewish New year, October, 1665, he revealed himself publicly in the synagogue as the Messiah, whereupon the mob shouted: "Long live our King, our Messiah!" Excitement and pandemonium reigned in Smyrna, and even moral restrictions were broken. Blasphemy knew no bounds, for the circulars of the Messiah read: "I, the Lord, your God, Sabbatai Zevi." He was declared the first-begotten son of God. It was not long, however, before the Turkish authorities demanded his presence at the capital in 1666. Upon arrival in Constantinople he was thrown into prison, but his followers continued in their perversion. Thousands visited him daily in the place of his confinement. Zevi died on the Day of Atonement in 1676, after he had been converted to the faith of Islam and had been able to bring many of his followers with him to his new faith. Of this base impostor a historian states that he "has secret adherents even to the present time."[34] Such impenetrable darkness of the spirit comes from the rejection of the true light.

If one considers the spiritual condition of Israel today, one finds no improvement over what has gone before. It appears that the present-day blindness of Israel (not that some of the elements were not present in former years as well) follows along certain definite lines. They are as follows: First, the nation exhibits a deplorable lack of spiritual perception of the Scriptures. It is not that they do not have reverence for the Holy Scriptures, for the Jews have not only counted all the verses of the Old Testament, the sum of all its letters, the middle verse and letter of every book, but they have watched over the Book with the greatest zeal and devotion. But because they fail to see the glorious center to which all Scripture proceeds and from which it again recedes is the Lord Jesus Christ, the spiritual message of the Word is closed to them.

---

[34] Ibid., 5:118.

Furthermore, they have so encased the Old Testament in rabbinical sophistries without number and in Talmudic regulations ad nauseam, that it is little wonder that spiritual perception is lacking. It is in this manner that the Jews—scattered among all the nations of the whole earth, weary and worn, persecuted and hated, reading their Scriptures in the Hebrew religiously every Sabbath—have contrived to keep the Old Testament complete and unimpaired without recognizing in it Him who is all its glory and beauty.[35]

Veiled Beliefs and Rituals

The letter is with them, as Paul testifies in 2 Corinthians 3, but the spiritual message is hidden from them. The apostle, after drawing a most clear and concise distinction between the Law and the Gospel of grace, reveals that the passing glory of the Law was hidden from Israel by the veil on Moses' face so that they could not look to the end of the dispensation of the Law which was to be abolished. *"But their minds were blinded: for until this day remaineth the same vail untaken away in the reading of the old testament; which vail is done away in Christ. But even unto this day, when Moses is read, the vail is upon their heart. Nevertheless when it [the heart] shall turn to the Lord, the vail shall be taken away"* (2 Corinthians 3:14-16, KJV).

That the veil is still upon the minds and hearts of the Jews is evident from a study of their tenets and practices. I choose first the orthodox Jew. On the night of the fourteenth of Nisan he performs the Passover ceremony (the *seder*). The table is set according to the rabbinical regulations. At the head of the table are placed three cakes of unleavened bread and, besides other elements, there is a plate set to one side containing the shank bone of a lamb, the Passover sacrifice. At a fixed time the father, or he who is conducting the ceremony, breaks the middle cake of unleavened bread from which all present eat. That half which is not eaten is hidden

---

[35] L. Gaussen, *Divine Inspiration of the Bible* (Grand Rapids: Kregel, 1971), p. 120.

away until after the meal (which takes place about the middle of the ceremony) is completed.

When it is brought forth again, it is no longer called *matsah* or unleavened bread, but bears the name of *aphikomen* (a transliteration of the aorist of the Greek word *aphikneomai* which means "to come forth from a place"). What a marvelous picture this ceremony is of the broken body of the second Person of the blessed Trinity, the burial of that body, and its coming forth from the grave! Yet Israel, though it sees Him not in it, so tenaciously clings to this ceremony, that Jewish fathers in Russia have been exiled to Siberia for performing this ceremony in the presence of their communistic children. Truly blindness has befallen Israel.

On the evening of the Day of Atonement the father (and the males of the household) takes a rooster and the mother (and her daughters) a hen and, waving the fowl above the head, say: "This is my atonement; this is my commutation. This rooster (or hen) shall go to death and I to life everlasting." What an absurd substitute for sin, for *"even Christ our passover is sacrificed for us,"* and *"He is the propitiation for our sins: and not for ours only, but also for the sins of the whole world"* (1 Corinthians 5:7; 1 John 2:2, KJV).

When the tenets of the Reformed Jews are considered, they have even less to commend them. First of all, contrary to the direct statement of Scripture, Reformed Jews claim that Israel's national existence came to an end when Jerusalem was destroyed by Titus in 70 A.D. The Jews are now only a religious and ethical group. They reject, moreover, the doctrine of the coming of a personal Messiah. In its stead they offer what they are pleased to call the "Messianic hope for the establishment of Truth, Justice, and Peace among all men."[36] They disclaim the biblical doctrine of the restoration of the Jews to Palestine.

Reformed Judaism illogically enough holds to the immortality of the soul, of which Scripture knows nothing, but

---

[36] J. W. Wise, *Liberalizing Liberal Judaism* (New York: Macmillan, 1924), p. 41.

abandons the doctrine of the immortality of the body. They have in particular after particular reversed the tenets of Rabbinic Judaism. Their sowing of the wind has brought them a harvest of the whirlwind, for their descendants are now drifting farther and farther from true Judaism. A remarkable example of this is to be found in the interesting book *Liberalizing Liberal Judaism* written by J. W. Wise, the son of the famous Rabbi Stephen S. Wise, wherein the author says that the purpose of religion is: "To help man to live well.... From the statement of the purpose of religion made above, it follows that its aim must not be to perpetuate itself."[37]

From a study of his book it becomes painfully evident that the Scriptures are a closed and sealed book to him. Religion is made a matter of utilitarianism garbled with some sociological and ethical principles. His contention with Liberal Judaism is that it is "unconscionable dogmatic," which he defines as "the ultra-positive assertion of God and the immortality of the soul!" Could such atheism be predicated of the darkest heathen? It is a true saying that the sun that melts the wax hardens the clay. How hardened has the heart of Israel become!

Before going on to another feature of this blindness, we will stop a moment to consider the text of 2 Corinthians 4:4 (KJV), which reads: *"The god of this world hath blinded the minds of them which believe not, lest the light of the glorious gospel of Christ, who is the image of God, should shine unto them."* Meyer believes that the apostle is speaking of "Gentiles and Jews, consequently in *ton apiston* no special reference to the Gentile character."[38] He is not alone in this. Some have concluded, therefore, that Romans 11:25 and 2 Corinthians 4:4 are both true of the nation Israel, attributing to them a double blindness (so Pettingill), whereas the Gentiles are under the blindness of 2 Corinthians 4:4 only. That Israel is doubly blinded I must strenuously and firmly deny,

---

[37] Ibid., pp. 18-19.
[38] H. A. Meyer, *Commentary on the New Testament* (New York: Funk & Wagnalls, 1884), p. 488.

for "Out of sixteen occurrences of the word *apistos* in the Pauline Epistles, fourteen are found in the Epistles to the Corinthians; it consistently means 'unbelieving,' and is always applied to the heathen, not to the Jews (except, perhaps Titus 1:15)."[39]

This states exactly my position in this matter. I believe that Romans 11:25 and 2 Corinthians 3:7-16 are referring to the same national blindness of Israel; 2 Corinthians 4:4 does not refer to Israel at all.

The blindness of Israel is further evident in their self-vindication and self-righteousness. In spite of the fact that the orthodox Jew confesses his sins in his daily prayers according to the Prayer Book, and confesses them more fully on the Day of Atonement, it is hard to find a more self-righteous man than he. He fails to see, when the Gospel is presented to him, that he is a sinner, because he does his best and treats his fellowman right. He is the direct spiritual descendant of the Pharisee of our Lord's day. Nor are the Liberal Jews any better.

Wise declares that the function of religion is not to establish arbitrarily a uniform standard of action, but to help each individual choose from any number of viewpoints and possibilities those which will best harmonize with "his own highest nature," so that he will make the choices which will best meet his particular problems.[40] This he declares in the face of the pronouncement of the psalmist in Psalm 14:1 (let alone Paul's indictment in Romans 1-3) that all men *"are corrupt, they have committed abominable deeds, there is no one who does good."* How well does his idea of man's "own highest nature" tally with Jeremiah's words, *"The heart is deceitful above all things, and desperately wicked: who can know it?"* (17:9, KJV).

Yet another feature of this blindness is the rejection of Jesus as Messiah. Of course, in a sense this is the fact of the

---

[39] J. H. Bernard, *Second Epistle to the Corinthians* (New York: Hodder & Stoughton, 1903), p. 60.
[40] J. W. Wise, *Liberalizing Liberal Judaism*, p. 53.

blindness itself (as is their lack of insight into the Scriptures), but it is treated here as a distinct characteristic of the present condition of the nation. The orthodox Jew will have nothing whatever to do with Jesus who is called the Christ. Nevertheless, he recites daily in the thirteen articles of his faith: "I believe with absolute faith in the coming of the Messiah, and, although He may tarry, in spite of this I shall wait for Him every day that comes."

Sometime ago a Jew of Warsaw, Poland, named Samuel Block announced on the Day of Atonement that he was going to fast until the Messiah came. He was a highly respected man, and many tried to swerve him from his announced purpose, but without avail. At the end of the first week he began to preach and showed great power and strength. Finally, he fell exhausted and whispered in his dying breath: "The Messiah is coming; I see Him!" But in spite of this longing for the Messiah and despite all the evidence from Scripture that Christ was truly that Messiah that should come into the world, He is persistently rejected.

The Reformed wing of Judaism, however, has not presented such a consistent picture. Having done away with the doctrine of the coming of a personal Messiah, they have now given themselves to an endless acclaim of Jesus as an ethical teacher, as one of the prophets, and as the greatest achievement of the Jews in the realm of religion. I quote from some of their statements.[41] Rabbi Gustav Gottheil claims:

> The question whether Jesus suffered martyrdom solely for His new teachings or for other causes, we will not discuss. The crown of thorns on His head makes Him only the more our Brother. For to this day it is borne by His people. Were He alive today, who, think you, would be nearest His heart, the persecuted or the persecutors?

---

[41] D. L. Cooper, *The Eternal God Revealing Himself* (Harrisburg, Pa.: Evangelical Press, 1928), pp. 347-48, 351.

James H. Hoffman, founder of the Hebrew Technical Institute of New York testifies:

> I recognize in Him the blending of the divine and the human, the lofty and the lowly, showing the path for the dual nature of man, by divine aspirations to gain the victory over the earthly life, tending to draw Him downwards—the Son of God triumphing over the child of the earth.

Rabbi Maurice H. Harris of New York exhorts:

> Let us not lose our Almighty Father in pantheistic vagueness [a timely warning], merging Him in nature; let us view Him as our Living Redeemer; our Saviour, for we often need to be saved—sometimes from the world, sometimes from ourselves.

With these statements even the more liberal Jews find fault. Wise claims it is not sufficient to claim that Jesus was a great spiritual and ethnical teacher; it must be sought out wherein this greatness lies and made available for the Jews in solving their problems. His own conclusion is that there are also problems in the life of Jesus, but these need not annoy the Jews, because "the whole question of his messiahship, of the unique incarnation in him of the spirit of God, of his perfection and sinlessness, and of his atonement and mediation for all men—all this the Jew can afford to ignore."[42] In short, he sets up a limited and feeble character which he expects the Jews to accept as their great Teacher. Well did Isaiah say of Israel: *"Sons I have reared and brought up, and they have revolted against me"* (Isaiah 1:2).

Stop for just a moment to contemplate the hatred of the Jews toward Hebrew Christians. Hating Jesus as they do, the Jews have transferred this enmity to His followers, especially

---

[42] J. W. Wise, *Liberalizing Liberal Judaism*, p. 119.

to those of Israel who have come to the light. When a Hebrew missionary goes to the Jews, he must be prepared to meet with an inordinate hatred, a groundless suspicion, and with all manner of abuse and calumny. How could they be expected to treat with kindness the followers of the One whom they hate? Any device that can be used by the rabbis to cast reproach on Hebrew believers and their missionary work is taken up and prosecuted to a degree worthy only of the accuser of the brethren. This hatred is analogous to that which Cain displayed toward Abel, and for the same reason: these have come to God with their own man-made religion, while the others have accepted the way God so graciously and mercifully offered.

The blindness of Israel is further seen in that they do not recognize their sin in rejecting Christ. In the confessions of the orthodox Jews (the Reformed feel they can omit this in their revised liturgy) there is mention made of almost every sin under the sun for recital on the Day of Atonement. But nowhere is there a recognition of the sin of rejecting the Messiah. We have translated from the Hebrew of the Jewish liturgy an interesting portion which is recited on the three great feasts: Passover, Pentecost, and Tabernacles.

> Because of our sins we have been exiled from our land and separated from our country, and we are not able to go up and worship before Thee, and to perform our duties in the house of Thy choice, in the great and holy house upon which Thy name is called, because of the hand stretched forth in Thy sanctuary. May it be favorable unto Thee, O God, our God, and the God of our fathers, merciful King, that Thou shalt return and have mercy upon us and upon Thy sanctuary in Thy great mercies, and shalt build it quickly and exalt its honor. Our Father, our King, reveal the honor of Thy kingdom upon us hastily, and appear and be exalted upon us in the sight of all living, and assemble our scattered ones from among the nations, and our

dispersed gather from the ends of the earth. And bring us to Zion Thy city with song and to Jerusalem, the house of Thy sanctuary, with everlasting joy, and there we shall make the offerings (sacrifices) of our duties continually according to their order and the additional sacrifices according to their law.[43]

Nowhere is mention made of the sin that separated them from the Temple of God, nor is its confession deemed necessary before Israel can rejoice with "everlasting joy." All her trials, sorrows, and persecutions Israel attributes to other causes than the real one.

Israel in her blindness has even gone farther. She claims that her exile and dispersion are means whereby she may fulfill her "mission to the world." Orthodox Jews have long given up this delusion, because they must feel keenly that they have no message for the world. But Reformed Judaism has stressed this tenet with a vengeance. Far from the scattering of Israel being considered a calamity, it should be looked upon, so they claim, as God's leading in their divinely appointed task. The time was when Rabbinic Judaism interpreted this mission to be the role Israel was playing as the suffering nation to atone for the sins of the world, according to the prophecy of Isaiah 53, but the liberal Jews have seen fit to interpret their mission as that in which they proclaim to the ends of the earth the unity of God, the prophets' ideals of justice and righteousness, and the era of peace and goodwill. The more liberal Jews, such as Wise, reject the whole conception of Israel's mission, because they deny that the ideals of the prophets were final or all-inclusive.

Finally, the hardening of Israel has manifest itself in their absolute ignorance of the nature and purpose of the Law. Because the Law is holy and just and spiritual, they contend that by so much it can render them so. They have preferred working out a righteousness of their own rather than to sub-

---

[43] M. Ginzburg and H. Levine, *Jewish Prayer Book*, p. 269.

mit to the righteousness of God, for *"Christ is the end of the law for righteousness to everyone who believes"* (Romans 10:4). The rabbis have conceived of the Law as an excellent system whereby man can find favor and merit with God. The regulations imposed by them upon the nation with this view in mind are sometimes downright absurd. We cite only one instance.

In the prohibitions of the Sabbath the rabbis ordained that if on the Sabbath a wall had fallen on a person, and it were doubtful whether he were under the ruins, whether he were alive or dead, a Jew or Gentile, it would be duty to clear away the rubbish sufficiently to find the body. If the person were not dead, the labor would have to be continued; but if he were dead, nothing further should be done to extricate the body. That the Law was given to bring them to Christ never occurred to Israel. They choose rather to use it as a means for attaining righteousness, although Paul tells us that *"if there had been a law given which could have given life, verily righteousness should have been by the law"* (Galatians 3:21, KJV).

If they had allowed themselves to be taught of God, they would have come to Christ as He so repeatedly declared (John 6:45). We have tried thus far to indicate the lines along which the hardening of Israel has proceeded. There is no necessity to multiply instances.

A Partial Blindness

One of the most important features of the subject of this study, the ignorance of which has caused more confusion and false notions among Christian people, is the partial character of Israel's blindness. Paul could not possibly be more explicit on this point than he is. First of all, he showed that all Israel never were the spiritual seed of Abraham. Faith in God alone, as in Abraham's case, is required of those who would be the spiritual seed. The apostle further explains that *"the election hath obtained it* [righteousness], *and the rest were blinded"* (Romans 11:7, KJV); only some of the branches were broken off. Only partial, not total, blindness has happened to Israel. What could be more clear than this? Yet there are those who try to discourage Jewish evangelization because they maintain Israel as a whole is blinded. I do not choose to be wise about that which is written. "Blindness in part" does not mean that all Israel has been partially blinded (so Calvin), nor does it imply that the blindness is partial as to time.

It means that there will be some in Israel who will not be blinded. God has always had a true witness to Himself from among Israel even in times of gravest apostasy. This faithful part is called the remnant in Scripture.

Looking at the whole of Israel's history, there are three distinct remnants: First, there was a remnant before Christ's advent. Up to the time of Elijah it appears as though the nation as a unit was bound to God, having the same sacrifices offered for them and having the same kings and judges over them. But after the nation as such had left God by going into apostasy, God revealed to Elijah that He had reserved to Himself 7,000 faithful followers. From that time till the coming of Christ and during His ministry (which was under the dispensation of Law), God had always had a number in Israel who were loyal to Him.[44] Of such were the disciples of the Lord and Simeon and Anna who were looking for God's salvation in Israel.

Second, there is a remnant of Israel in this Church age. Paul, in speaking of the remnant in Elijah's day, adds another proof that God has not totally rejected nor blinded Israel by stating that *"there has also come to be at the present time a remnant according to God's gracious choice"* (Romans 11:5). Here is the election within the election of which I have previously spoken. The difference, however, between the present remnant and the preceding, as well as the following one, is that the remnant of this age belongs no longer to the commonwealth of Israel, but is one with all believers in Christ Jesus. He has come to God just as the Gentile, for *"the*

---

[44] Sanday and Headlam, *Romans*, p. 316.

same Lord is...abounding in riches for all who call upon Him" (Romans 10:12).

During the national rejection of Israel God has made it possible that through an offer of the Gospel and its acceptance, any individual Israelite can be saved. In the Church there is only one way of entrance for Jew and Gentile: through faith in Christ's redeeming work; only one standing: "accepted in the beloved"; and only one destination: heavenly glory in the presence of Christ forever. Finally, there is yet to be another remnant, but of this I speak more particularly later.

Let us now consider briefly the purpose of Israel's blindness. No doubt many children of God have looked upon the hardening of the chosen people as a divine judgment pure and simple. Such it has been, but it has meant more than that. The apostle Paul reveals that *"by their transgression salvation has come to the Gentiles, to make them jealous"* (Romans 11:11). God had planned only one way of saving men, and to accomplish this He placed Jew and Gentile "under sin," after having set aside Israel's privileges as a means to salvation, so that both would have to be saved by grace through faith. Furthermore, the coming of salvation to the "sinners of the Gentiles" was to provoke Israel to jealousy. How different has been the result because of the cruel treatment Israel has received at the hands of professing Christendom. Their casting away has meant the reconciling of the world.

The End of Israel's Blindness

What remains now is to consider the end of Israel's blindness. This is the restricted and circumscribed field of the mystery, for it was never known until Paul revealed it in Romans 11:25-27. God had revealed to the Old Testament prophets that a hardening would befall Israel and that it would be partial in its scope, but it had never been made known when this blindness would end. So Paul states:

"For I would not, brethren, that ye should be ignorant of this mystery, lest ye should be wise in your own conceits; that blindness in part is happened to Israel, UNTIL THE FULNESS OF THE GENTILES BE COME IN. And so all Israel shall be saved: as it is written, There shall come out of Sion the Deliverer, and shall turn away ungodliness from Jacob: For this is my covenant unto them, when I shall take away their sins."   (Romans 11:25-27, KJV)

What does Paul mean by the clause "until the fulness of the Gentiles be come in"? The word "until" is here used as a subordinate conjunction denoting the time up to which the blindness will continue. There are many opinions as to the meaning of "the fulness of the Gentiles" (*to pleroma ton ethnon*). To show the diversity of opinion on this point I mention some of the views of commentators on this text. Sanday and Headlam maintain that *to pleroma* refers to the Gentile world as a whole. Griffith Thomas refers the time to the close of the Gentile dispensation. Faber, Stifler, Brookes, and Chalmers are all of the opinion that the time referred to is identical with "the times of the Gentiles." Godet, after denoting "the fulness of the Gentiles" as the totality of the Gentile nations, designates the time as "the times of the Gentiles."

Bosworth contends that reference is made to the large majority of the Gentile population of the world, while Govett thinks the phrase refers to the elect of this dispensation out of all nations. Moule holds that *eiselthe* ("be come in") refers to a time when the ingathering of the Gentile children of God will not be at an end, but running high.

With such variance of opinion it would be presumptuous to be dogmatic. Our conviction is, however, that "the fulness of the Gentiles" refers to all the elect of this Church age, from the Gentiles "a people for his name" and from the Jews "a remnant according to the election of grace." In a word, it is the Church. We hold further, as does Dr. Scofield, that "the fulness of the Gentiles" and "the times of the Gentiles" are

not synonymous. Our reason for believing so is found in the
fact that the former is an ecclesiastical designation and the
latter is a political designation, speaking of the world monar-
chies from the time of Nebuchadnezzar till the rule of Antichrist. These two phrases do not have the same terminus in
point of time. The first ends at the rapture; the second is sud-
denly brought to a close by the revelation of Christ in great
power and glory.

This concludes our contemplation of Israel's present. I well
remember the sad but true words of my former Hebrew professor in a grammar class when he said: "Our nation Israel is
like the Hebrew language. It has a past tense and a future
tense but no present."[45]

ISRAEL'S FUTURE: RESTORED

Against the background of Israel's present, her future
shines forth the more graciously, if the word of Scripture is to
be trusted. The subject for our present consideration is to
contemplate how God will bring about the restoration of
Israel. In our former study of Daniel's seventy weeks I attempted to show that the Jewish age was brought to a sudden
close at the end of the sixty-ninth week with the cutting off of
Messiah the Prince. When the Church age is brought to a
close by the completion of the Body of Christ from Jews and
Gentiles, the blindness will be taken away from Israel
(Romans 11:25), and the Jewish clock will again begin to tick.
The Law will again be in force, part of the nation Israel will
be regathered in unbelief to Palestine, and the Temple will be
rebuilt. This period is known as the Great Tribulation which
intervenes between "the fulness of the Gentiles" and the time
when "all Israel shall be saved."

---

[45] In spoken Hebrew, the present tense is omitted; the simple active participle
takes its place.

The Events in the Great Tribulation

The cause of the Great Tribulation is threefold: moral, satanic, political.[46] The failure of Israel to accept her Messiah and the complete moral failure on the part of Gentile nations and professing Christendom will bring on this period (Ezekiel 30:3). Second, it will be occasioned by the increase in the power and influence of Satan in preparing for the time when he shall reveal his man of sin as the god of the age (2 Thessalonians 2:7-8) in the middle of the period. In the third place, it will be occasioned by the plan of God to set His King on His holy hill of Zion.

There will be certain distinct groups in this time of the Great Tribulation. That Israel is particularly in view can be seen from Jeremiah 30:4-7 where the prophet foretells of a day when there will be heard a voice of trembling, of fear, and not peace, when every man will have his hands on his loins as a woman in travail with his face turned to paleness, because *"it is the time of Jacob's distress."* All the nations will form a second company, for Jeremiah testifies again in 25:31 that God has a *"controversy with the nations,"* while Ezekiel speaks (30:3) of a *"time for the nations."* Apostate Christendom (the bad fish and tares of Matthew 13) will be included in mystery Babylon, which consists of all the false religious systems of all ages.

Finally, there will be the Tribulation remnant of Israel of which I spoke cursorily above. To ascertain the constituency and purpose of this remnant we turn our attention now to chapter 7 of the Book of Revelation where two groups are discernible: the 144,000 and the great multitude from all nations, kindreds, peoples, and tongues. Milligan is of the opinion that the 144,000 sealed ones refer primarily to Jewish Christians, but have a wider application as well in the Church universal. The difficulty of the Jewish names he dispenses with by claiming that it is customary for John to "heighten and spiritualize all Jewish names." His final conclusion upon

---

[46] N. B. Harrison, *His Sure Return* (Chicago: Book Center, 1926), pp. 33-46.

this chapter is that the two companies are identical, in the one case being sealed as God's own and in the second instance having entered into the peace and joy of their Lord.[47]

Alford sees in the 144,000 all the elect of God who will be living on earth at the coming of the Lord, "symbolical of the first-fruits of the church." He contends that the groups in this chapter are not identical, but that the first is included in the second. He explains further that "out of great tribulation" means "the whole sum of the trials of the saints of God."[48]

I accept neither of these statements as being adequate to explain all the facts in the case. In the first place, the Church is not in view in the Book of Revelation (except as seated in heaven viewing the events upon the earth) from chapter 4 through 19. In the second place, I find it difficult to accept any interpretation that views the names of the Jewish tribes as to spiritualize them into the Israel of God or the Church universal. I am in hearty agreement with that maxim of interpretation which states: "When the plain sense makes good sense, seek no other sense." On this principle we should interpret the book of Revelation, as far as possible, literally. This would lead us to conclude concerning the 144,000 sealed ones that when the Church is caught up to be with the Lord, God will call a remnant of His people to proclaim the Gospel of the Kingdom, for *"this gospel of the kingdom shall be preached in all the world for a witness unto all nations; and then shall the end come"* (Matthew 24:14, KJV). I continue with a splendid statement of Dr. Gaebelein:

> This remnant, enlightened by the Holy Spirit, will pass through the entire seven years. Many of them will suffer martyrdom [Revelation 20:4], but the greater part will pass through the entire tribulation, enduring to the end, and then saved [delivered] by their King,

---

[47] W. Milligan, *The Book of Revelation* (New York: Armstrong, 1903), pp. 116, 118, 130.
[48] H. Alford, *Alford's Greek Testament* (Grand Rapids: Guardian Press, 1976), 4:624, 628.

our Lord, when He comes in glory. The so-called orthodox Jews will probably constitute with members of the other tribes [ten tribes] this remnant.[49]

The truth of this remnant is brought out in many Old Testament passages and explains the existence and purpose of the imprecatory psalms. (Remnant passages: Psalm 44:10-26; 55-57; 64; 79; 80; Isaiah 63:15; 64.) The result of this testimony is seen in the great multitude of Gentiles saved.

The Outcome of the Great Tribulation

Let us now look at the character and consequences of the Great Tribulation. From Isaiah 24 to 28 and from Revelation 8 to 19, an idea of the characteristics of this period may be gained. (Also Joel, Zephaniah, and most of the other prophets.) There will be world-wide woe, universal distress, and unprecedented anguish. Fear and terror will reign supreme. The earth will reel, rock, and shake, so that its very foundations will be moved. God will by grievous judgments melt the nations and Israel in a fiery furnace. It will no doubt be a period of trial, sorrow, calamity, spiritual darkness, wickedness, and catastrophe such as the world has never seen nor imagined (Matthew 24:32; Daniel 12:1; 2 Peter 3:3; Luke 18:7; John 9:4; and others).

The plagues of Egypt will be insignificant as compared to it (if we are to understand Revelation literally at all), and the Reign of Terror in France during the French Revolution with its unspeakable atrocities and abominations will not even remotely approximate it. The result of this period for Israel as a nation will be that she will emerge purified *"as silver is refined"* and *"as gold is tested"* (Zechariah 13:9). A great multitude will be saved from all nations. The beast and the false prophet will be cast into the lake of fire and Satan will be bound for a thousand years.

---

[49] A. C. Gaebelein, *The Revelation* (Neptune, N.J.: Loizeaux, 1961), p. 58.

Israel's full restoration will consist in her regathering, conversion, and future blessedness. Those who are watching the
events of the day can see that God is preparing Israel for an
even greater regathering. The hands of the clock of
Palestine's progress are moving so quickly that it is easy to
find oneself citing facts and figures that are out of date. In
1891 Dr. J. H. Brookes stated in his book *Till He Come*:
"From twenty to fifty Jewish families are landed every week
at Jaffa."[50] Present figures compare with his as a river to a
stream.

The population of the State of Israel increased from 24,000
to 2,561,400 between 1882 and 1970. When the State of Israel
was established in 1948, there were only 650,000 Jews in the
Holy Land. In 1970 Oriental Jews were in the majority. Jews
of American and European origin comprised 48 percent of
the population and second generation Israelis comprised 8
percent. Almost 13,000 Jews emigrated from the USSR in
1971, compared to 5,675 in the previous four years. On
January 11, 1972, the Jewish population of Israel passed the
three million mark. (Emigration from Russia was an outstanding element through the year.) Emigration in 1972 was
56,000, an increase of 34 percent over 1971. Of the new-
comers 70 percent were from Europe, 20 percent from the
Americas, and only 10 percent from Asia and Africa. The
majority (68 percent) were between fifteen and sixty years of
age; 23 percent were children fourteen years old and under; 9
percent were over sixty. Emigration from the Americas and
Western Europe declined, yet 30,000 (more than half the total
and twice as many as in 1971) came from the Soviet Union,

---

[50] J. H. Brookes, *Till He Come* (Chicago: Gospel Publ., 1891), p. 86. *American Jewish Year Book, 1945-46* (47:636) indicates the Jewish population in Palestine was 12,000 in 1839; 35,000 in 1880; 70,000 in 1900; 83,794 in 1922; and 175,610 in 1931. The estimate for 1943 was 502,912; and for 1944, 521,564. According to the *American Jewish Year Book, 1950* (51:407), the Jewish population was 713,000 in Nov. 1948 and 891,000 in May 1949. In 1949 the ultramodern Tel Aviv alone had a population of over 300,000. See *A Christian Report of Israel, May 1949*, p. 1, by the American Christian Palestine Committee Study Tour to Israel. Also see *American Jewish Year Book, 1972*, pp. 567-68; *Britannica Book of the Year, 1973*, pp. 383-84; and *American Jewish Year Book, 1973*, p. 502.

one-third from the region (or republic) of Soviet Georgia. It was estimated that about 100,000 more Russian Jews had applied for permission to emigrate. The estimated population of Israel for 1977 was 3,610,000 (another estimate sets it at 3,695,600) with the largest percentage in the 15-59 bracket— 55.8 percent.[51]

Is God "finished" with Israel? Never! But these facts of history only corroborate the word of Scripture. Moses foretold a literal scattering of Israel, but he also predicted just as literal a regathering. He predicted of Israel: *"'The* LORD *your God will restore you from captivity, and have compassion on you, and will gather you again from all the peoples where the* LORD *your God has scattered you'"* (Deuteronomy 30:3).

When I attempt to give the prophetic testimony on this point I am convinced that an *embarras de richesse* is our lot. I quote only the passage in Isaiah 11:11-12 (KJV):

> *"And it shall come to pass in that day, that the Lord shall set his hand again the second time to recover the remnant of his people, which shall be left, from Assyria, and from Egypt, and from Pathros, and from Cush, and from Elam, and from Shinar, and from Hamath, and from the islands of the sea. And he shall set up an ensign for the nations, and shall assemble the outcasts of Israel, and gather together the dispersed of Judah from the four corners of the earth."*

Some try to dissipate the force of this prophecy by maintaining that it has reference to the return from Babylon. This is untenable because the phrases "the second time" and "from the four corners of the earth" would be inexplicable. All the prophets are at one in declaring a regathering (worldwide) of Israel before the millennial reign of Christ. Finally, Christ Himself places His word of prophecy in support of this truth. In describing the condition of Israel during and immediately

---

[51] *The World Almanac*, 1979, p. 548.

after the Great Tribulation, He declared: *"'And He* [speaking of His own coming in glory] *will send forth His angels with a great trumpet and they will gather together His elect from the four winds, from one end of the sky to the other'"* (Matthew 24:31). No child of God need fear for Israel's regathering, because the Lord hath purposed it and it shall stand.

The regathering of Israel will precede her conversion. She will be saved in the same manner that the apostle Paul was saved: by a direct revelation of the Lord Jesus Christ from glory. Before Paul makes the definite prophecy in Romans 11:26 concerning Israel's conversion, he gives intimations of it beforehand. He asks: *"Now if the fall of them be the riches of the world...how much more their fulness?"* (Romans 11:12, KJV). Again he asks: *"For if the casting away of them be the reconciling of the world, what shall the receiving of them be, but life from the dead?"* (Romans 11:15, KJV). (I understand this to refer, not to "the resurrection of the dead, which will introduce the new Messianic age,"[52] but to the national resurrection spoken of by Ezekiel in chapter 37 of his prophecy.) Yet once more Paul reveals that *"they also, if they do not continue in their unbelief, will be grafted in"* (Romans 11:23). He is speaking here of grafting into the good olive tree which is the Abrahamic Covenant, the root of the tree being Abraham. It is impossible that the olive tree be the Church, for how, then, could Paul exhort and warn: *"Continue in his goodness; otherwise thou also shalt be cut off"* (Romans 11:22, KJV)? No one who has truly been baptized by the Holy Spirit into the body of Christ can ever be separated from Him.

After these inferential statements the apostle foretells: *"And so all Israel shall be saved: as it is written, There shall come out of Sion the Deliverer, and shall turn away ungodliness from Jacob"* (Romans 11:26, KJV). This is Israel's conversion when they look upon Him whom they have pierced,

---

[52] E. I. Bosworth, *Commentary on Romans* (New York: Macmillan, 1919), p. 216.

and mourn for Him as for an only son. "All Israel" refers to those Jews living at the coming of Christ in power to earth after the rebels have been purged out (Ezekiel 20:35-38). It is most assuredly not synonymous with "every Israelite" who has ever lived.

When Israel is saved, the ratification of the New Covenant (Jeremiah 31:31; Romans 11:27; Hebrews 8:7-13) will take place. Israel is definitely to be saved by the Lord with an everlasting salvation, all the theories of the higher critics and the effervescings of those who believe not God to the contrary notwithstanding! What a glorious future is Israel's! Do we rejoice with her on account of it, or do we begrudge her all her promised blessings while leaving her all the curses? And it is just at this point that I wish to draw a distinction — it may appear irrelevant — between the defection and apostasy of Israel and that of Christendom. The former is never complete, because there is always the promise of future restoration and conversion; the latter is irreparable because it ends with the overthrow of mystery Babylon. It is well to remember this when we are prone to dwell unduly on Israel's unfaithfulness.

Just as Israel scattered means Israel persecuted and blinded, so Israel regathered means Israel converted and blessed. The Jews as a nation will be blessed and made a blessing. In the first place, their presence in the land will mean blessing for them because, in the case of Israel, blessing has always been inextricably bound up with occupancy of the land. We are being given a distinct preview of this in the condition of Palestine today. In 1920 the export of oranges from Palestine amounted to less than 1,000,000 cases. By 1933 it was over 4,000,000 cases. A total of 4,500,000 cases of oranges were sent to Europe during the 1948-49 season. The chief crops continue to be citrus fruits, grains, olives, fruits, grapes, figs, cotton, vegetables. For the year 1978-79, a look at the entire cultivated area of Israel showed 2,800 dunams were under field crops, 390 under vegetables, potatoes, pumpkins, and melons, 875 under citrus and orchards, 56 under fish ponds, and 189 under various crops, including auxiliary farms, nurseries, and flowers. Oranges produced in 1977 came to 897 metric tons.[53] How the land will flow with milk and honey when converted Israel will be settled there! It is a matter of common knowledge that the land of Palestine has never been entirely occupied by the chosen people. The land grant of Genesis 15:18 calls for a stretch of land of 300,000 square miles or twelve and one-half times the size of Great Britain and Ireland. When it is occupied, *"each of them will sit under his vine and under his fig tree, with no one to make them afraid, for the mouth of the* LORD *of hosts has spoken"* (Micah 4:4).

Second, Israel will be blessed by the presence of the King. Who can fully tell forth all the blessing that will flow from the immediate and direct reign of the righteous King? This is a theme upon which the Old Testament prophets so loved to dwell. Jeremiah prophesied that the days were coming when the Lord would raise up unto David a righteous Branch and a King who would reign and prosper, executing judgment and justice in the earth. Isaiah testified that *"of the increase of his government and peace there shall be no end, upon the throne of David, and upon his kingdom, to order it, and to establish it with judgment and with justice from henceforth even for ever"* (9:7, KJV). Israel (and the nations as well) has sighed and yearned for the day when justice and judgment would be established in the earth, but it is possible only through the reign of the Lord our righteousness. Blessed indeed will be that people whose God and King is the Lord.

But Israel will not enjoy her blessings alone, for she will be used of God to bless all the nations of the earth during the Millennium. By a Temple ritual and system of sacrifices she will show forth commemoratively the wonders of the death of

[53] *American Jewish Year Book, 1950,* 51:404. Export of goods amounted to more than $730 million net in 1970, which was 6 percent higher than in 1969 and 47 percent more than in 1967. Industry accounted for 84 percent of the goods exported, which included 35 percent polished diamonds, 10 percent citrus, and 6 percent other farm produce (*Facts About Israel,* Jerusalem, 1972, p. 98). See also *The World Almanac,* 1979, p. 548, and *Encylopaedia Britannica, 1979 Book of the Year,* pp. 459-460.

her King and Lord, even as she unknowingly did by way of anticipation in Old Testament times. These sacrifices will be to her what the Lord's Supper is to believers now. There is no hint that Israel will perform this ritual because she sets aside or disclaims the death of Christ on Calvary, for by it she has been saved upon His second appearing. Furthermore, Israel will publish over the whole earth the truth of God. The nations will be brought to God through Israel and not through the Church. The church's task is to preach the Gospel of grace, so that a people from among the Gentiles and the remnant from Israel may accept Christ as Saviour and Lord. Isaiah told Israel: *"And nations will come to your light, and kings to the brightness of your rising"* (Isaiah 60:3).

Throughout the Scriptures the order is unmistakable: the conversion of Israel, then that of the nations. First, it will be Israel saying: "God be merciful unto us, and bless us"; and then it will be "God shall bless us; and all the ends of the earth shall fear Him." The shortest psalm in the psalter bears out this truth. Again note the order: *"O praise the LORD, all ye nations: praise him, all ye people. For his merciful kindness is great toward us [lit., has conquered us]: and the truth of the LORD endureth for ever"* (Psalm 117, KJV). Then it will be *"that ten men shall take hold out of all languages of the nations, even shall take hold of the skirt of him that is a Jew, saying, We will go with you; for we have heard that God is with you"* (Zechariah 8:23, KJV). Who but eternal, gracious, merciful, and adorable God the Father could have planned such an ineffably glorious future for Israel? Little wonder it is, then, that Paul, who at first with aching and sorrowing heart depicted Israel's rejection, then the final consummation of God's plan wherein he saw that *"God hath concluded them all in unbelief, that he might have mercy upon all"* (Romans 11:32, KJV), little wonder it is, I say, that the apostle breaks forth in such a paean:

> *"O the depth of the riches both of the wisdom and knowledge of God! how unsearchable are his judg-*

*ments, and his ways past finding out! For who hath
known the mind of the Lord? or who hath been his
counsellor? Or who hath first given to him, and it
shall be recompensed unto him again? For of him,
and through him, and to him, are all things: to whom
be glory for ever. Amen."*   (Romans 11:33-36, KJV)

CONCLUSION

In view of all that we have considered, it appears that the
believer's duty to Israel is threefold. First, he should love
them with a pure love fervently, for they are still beloved of
God for the fathers' sake. Second, he should try by the
strength of the Spirit to provoke them, not to anger, hatred,
or indifference, but to jealousy because of the manifestation
of the blessedness of belonging to Christ and serving the true
and living God. Third, he should strive by as much as is in
him, the Lord helping and leading, to give the Gospel to the
Jew, and in God's order: "to the Jew first." Most Christians
are willing to subscribe to the first two parts of this duty to
Israel, but they have many objections to the third part. A
favorite pretext is that Israel has had her day of opportunity.
Has any other nation done any better with their day of
privilege?

Furthermore, Paul proves conclusively in Romans 10 that
the Gospel is to be preached to Jew and Gentile alike. Others
say the Jews are past hope of redemption. This displays a
most irreverent minimizing of the power of the Father to
draw, of the Spirit to convict, and of the Son to save. Probably the worst objection is: "Jesus Christ Himself when on
earth could not convert them." This shows a woeful ignorance of the Scriptures, for after Christ's rejection by Israel,
He announced God's hidden purpose to call out the Church
by His death and resurrection. Christ fulfilled all that He
came to do. He fully accomplished the work that the Father
had given Him to do. Israel was not converted under Christ's

ministry, but neither will the Gentiles come to God under the Spirit's ministry. Moreover, the unbelief of Israel is no more reason for turning from them than the unbelief of the Gentiles should cause us to abandon them.

It is a sad comment on the history of the Church that she has forgotten that her formation under God was brought about by Jewish missions to Gentiles.[54] Gratitude should spur her on to give the Gospel to the Jews. Such an attitude as that taken by Martin Luther should never be countenanced by her. He said: "A Jewish heart is so stock-stone-devil-iron-hard, that in no wise can it be moved; they are young devils; damned to hell; to convert these devil's brats (as some fondly ween out of the Epistle to the Romans) is impossible."[55] Luther evidently forgot for the time that there always has been a blessing attached to the Jews, directly or indirectly. "Their rejection brought blessing to the Gentiles, and their restoration will bring blessing to the world."[56] God's order now is "to the Jew first," not a matter of preeminence but of order. *"O . . . ye that make mention of the* LORD, *keep not silence, and give him no rest, till he establish, and till he make Jerusalem a praise in the earth"* (Isaiah 62:6-7, KJV).

---

[54] P. Mauro, *A Study of Romans* (Boston: Hamilton, 1914), p. 101.
[55] R. V. Foster, *Romans*, p. 324.
[56] W.H.G. Thomas, *St. Paul's Epistle to the Romans* (Grand Rapids: Eerdmans, 1950), p. 295.

Part 6

ISRAEL IN ALL THE SCRIPTURES

14

Why God Needs Israel

WE OFTEN HEAR people speak of what God means to Israel, and this is eminently scriptural. In his closing address to his people, Moses had been constrained of the Spirit of God to say: *"The eternal God is a dwelling place, and underneath are the everlasting arms"* (Deuteronomy 33:27). In the prayer of Moses found in Psalm 90 are these words: *"Lord, Thou hast been our dwelling place in all generations"* (Psalm 90:1). So we could multiply Scriptures to show what God means to Israel.

But how many have ever heard what Israel means to God? Yet this is a truth which has ample proof in Scripture also. Let us note first the inception of the nation. The failure of Adam is known to everyone who has read the Bible and to many who have not. The sin and crime of Cain is also written large on the sacred page. Nor was the generation of Noah one whit better, until God saw He must destroy the whole earth by a great deluge. The Flood, however, did not put an end to the failure of the human race, for soon we find men devising plans whereby they might build a city and make a name for themselves.

God in His righteous judgment confounded the language of the race and scattered His creatures over the face of the whole earth. From this great mass of human wreckage and sin God called one man, Abraham, and His first promise to him was (and most significant it is too): *"'I will make you a great nation.'"* Before God ever promised to bless him or make his name great, He covenanted that out of the man of His sovereign choice, there should issue a nation. But this gracious promise seemed impossible of fulfillment on the human side because of the advanced age of both Sarah and Abraham. So God performed a miracle to bring into existence the miracle nation, Israel.

God, then, had purposed to use a nation as the channel of His purposes in the earth. Nothing could be more clear than this from a study of the very structure of the book of Genesis, the seed plot of the entire Word of God. In eleven chapters God occupies Himself with the story of the creation of the material world, the creation of man, the entrance of sin into the world, the Flood, the propagation of the race, the beginning of nations, the multiplication of languages, and the diffusion of the race over the earth. In the remaining thirty-nine chapters of Genesis God is engaged in setting forth the inception, growth, and expansion of but one nation from its progenitor, Abraham. Surely there is divine wisdom here as in all His works, for God reveals that He intends to use the nation for His purposes.

When we thus consider the origin of this miracle nation and then further note its history and God's dealings with it throughout the centuries, we are constrained to say that Israel means a great deal to God. Furthermore, we are emboldened to assert—and we do it with all reverence—that God, since He has condescended to use secondary means and agents, has needed and does need Israel for several specific purposes. What are these purposes?

For a Witness and Service

First, God needed Israel—and these are the reasons Israel means much to God—to witness to the unity of God. All the highly concocted views of the destructive critics to the contrary notwithstanding, Israel never had an evolution in its faith from a supposedly original animism, totemism, or polytheism. There never was a time in the history of Israel, even during the periods of her greatest declensions, when she was unaware of the fact that she had been called by the true and the living God, and not by a multiplicity of gods.

To us in the twentieth century, this may appear but a small or unnecessary task for a nation, but it serves only to show how far we are removed from the times and conditions of the patriarchs. At the time of Abraham, or even later in the time of the kings of Israel and Judah, witnessing to the unity of God was not analogous to carrying coal to Newcastle. Even today, when the truth of monotheism has long held its place in the minds of men, there is a need of witnessing to the unity of the living God in view of the countless heathen who are worshiping their gods. But even in so-called enlightened countries there is a crying need to stress the one true God, when one is informed that in their chapels in France today men are worshiping Satan, the opposer of God. In America we have something almost as bad in the American Association for the Advancement of Atheism.

But Israel, although many have been their departures from God, have always testified to this calling of theirs. To this day the national motto of Israel is: "Hear, O Israel: Jehovah our God is one Jehovah." They have kept in mind the words of Isaiah: *"'You are My witnesses,' declares the* LORD, *'and My servant whom I have chosen, in order that you may know and believe Me, and understand that I am He. Before Me there was no God formed, and there will be none after Me. I, even I, am the* LORD; *and there is no savior besides me'"* (43:10-11). This passage certainly reveals two facts: Israel is God's witness and the witness is to the person of God.

Ever since the return from Babylon, Israel could not be accused of idolatry or the worship of more than one God. Every orthodox Jew in his daily prayers in the synagogue or at home recites at the conclusion of his praying the thirteen articles of faith drawn up by Maimonides, the great Jewish rabbi and philosopher of the Middle Ages. The second article of faith reads thus: "I believe with a complete faith that the Creator, blessed be His name, is One and there is no unity like Him in any manner whatsoever, and He alone is our God who was, who is, and who shall be."

Israel was meant not only to witness to the unity of God, but they were intended by God to show the blessedness of serving God.

This thought was in the mind of Moses when he commanded Israel after this fashion: *"'See, I have taught you statutes and judgments just as the* LORD *my God commanded me, that you should do thus in the land where you are entering to possess it. So keep and do them, for that is your wisdom and your understanding in the sight of the peoples who will hear all these statutes, and say, "Surely this great nation is a wise and understanding people." For what great nation is there that has a god so near to it as is the* LORD *our God whenever we call on Him? Or what great nation is there that has statutes and judgments as righteous as this whole law which I am setting before you today?'"* (Deuteronomy 4:5-8).

Moses closed his public ministry to Israel with these recorded words:

"'There is none like the God of Jeshurun, who rides the heavens to your help, and through the skies in His majesty. The eternal God is a dwelling place, and underneath are the everlasting arms; and He drove out the enemy from before you, and said, "Destroy!" So Israel dwells in security, the fountain of Jacob secluded, in a land of grain and new wine; His heavens also drop down dew. Blessed are you, O Israel; who is like you, a people saved by the LORD, *who is the shield of your help, and the sword of your majesty! So your enemies shall cringe before you, and you shall tread upon their high places'"* (Deuteronomy 33:26-29).

As long as Israel remained in the path of God's will and served Him, they were an example to all the surrounding nations and to us of how God will bless such. When God wanted to show how He could bless those who serve Him, He took the nation Israel to exhibit it on a national scale.

For the Sake of the Scriptures

But God needed Israel for more than these purposes already outlined; He purposed to use them in the reception, preservation, and transmission of the Scriptures. The nation had explicit instructions for the preservation of the words of God: *"'And these words, which I am commanding you today, shall be on your heart; and you shall teach them diligently to your sons and shall talk of them when you sit in your house and when you walk by the way and when you lie down and when you rise up. And you shall bind them as a sign on your hand and they shall be as frontals on your forehead. And you shall write them on the doorposts of your house and on your gates'"* (Deuteronomy 6:6-9). To this day, these specific injunctions are kept. Parents are diligent in teaching their children the sacred Scriptures that have been handed down to them.

They also place these words upon their hands and between their eyes in the use of phylacteries, the praying paraphernalia of the orthodox Jews which has portions of Scripture encased in leather which are bound around the left hand and around the forehead. And the third command is kept in placing *mezuzoth* (small wooden or metal receptacles with the portion of Scripture from Deuteronomy 6:6-9) upon the doorposts of the house. In other ways also Israel has preserved the sacred text, so that today scholars still marvel at the wonderful preservation of the Hebrew text. Paul, you remember, considered this one of the advantages of the nation: *"Then what advantage has the Jew? Or what is the benefit of circumcision? Great in every respect. First of all, that they were entrusted with the oracles of God"* (Romans 3:1-2).

Throughout the centuries, moreover, Israel has shown to the world the sustaining power of the Scriptures. I do not argue that Israel has always been obedient to the Word, but even during the times of her disobedience, she has manifested how capable the Scriptures are of sustaining. This devotion to the Word has kept Israel buoyed up through the centuries when persecutions, that would have broken the morale of the mightest of nations, came upon them like an overwhelming flood. It is as though God had said: "I desire to show to the world how powerful my Word is to sustain, even though not always followed, and I choose Israel to convey this message to the world."

Does not Israel mean much to God in this way? The thought we have been dwelling upon is well brought out by a poem from the pen of Chaim Nachman Bialik (1873-1934), one of the greatest of Hebrew poets. The poem is all the more wonderful when we consider that the poet was not a believer in the Lord Jesus Christ. (We take the liberty of changing one word in the last line: "Talmud's" to the word "Bible's").

"THE SOURCE OF STRENGTH"

And shouldest thou wish to know the source
From which thy tortured brethren drew
In evil days their strength of soul
To meet their doom: stretch out their necks
To each uplifted knife and axe,
In flames, on stakes to die with joy,
And with a whisper, "God is one"
To close their lips?
Then enter thou the House of God,
The House of Study, old and gray,
Throughout the sultry summer days,
Throughout the gloomy winter nights,
At morning, midday, or at eve;
Perchance there is a remnant yet,
Perchance thy eye may still behold
In some dark corner, hid from view,
A cast-off shadow of the past,
The profile of some pallid face,
Upon an ancient folio bent,
Who seeks to drown unspoken woes,
In the (Bible's) boundless waves.

Many a time has it been my privilege to see this very thing in the synagogue. Multitudes upon multitudes in Israel have said and could say with the psalmist: *"This is my comfort in my affliction, that Thy word has revived me."* Again, *"If Thy law had not been my delight, then I would have perished in my affliction"* (Psalm 119:50, 92).

For the Channel of Messiah

In addition to what has been indicated above, God needed Israel as a channel for the Messiah, for He so purposed to bring the Saviour into the world. When God promised the woman in the Garden of Eden that of her seed would come the great Deliverer, the promise was most general, for He could have come from any group or nation of the human race. But with the call of Abraham, God made it very clear that in Abraham's seed would all the nations of the earth be blessed. Paul explains this in Galatians 3 as referring to the Messiah.

With the passage of time the promises with regard to Him became more and more circumscribed and more and more detailed. Note the narrowing down of the predictions: first it was the seed of the woman, then Abraham's seed, then Isaac's seed, then Jacob's seed, then the tribe of Judah, and finally, the house and lineage of David. If one has intelligently read the Old Testament, by the time he reaches Matthew 1:1 where he reads: *"The book of the genealogy of Jesus Christ, the son of David, the son of Abraham,"* he visualizes in his mind the appearance of One who is of the human race, of the royal line of David, One to be born in Bethlehem of Judea, and of a virgin of some branch of David's house other than that of the rejected and despised Coniah (Jeremiah 22:24-30).

Such was Christ: He alone of all who have walked the earth fulfilled all the blueprint specifications for the Messiah explicitly laid down in the Old Testament Scriptures. And He was of the nation Israel. Truly, Israel must mean much to God when He found that He could use them as the channel for the incarnation of His own ever blessed and well-beloved and only begotten Son. Paul enumerated the blessings of Israel in this manner: *"Israelites, to whom belongs the adoption as sons and the glory and the covenants and the giving of the Law and the temple service and the promises, whose are the fathers, and from whom is the Christ according to the flesh, who is over all, God blessed forever. Amen"* (Romans 9:4-5). He, the Christ of God, is the climax and the capstone of all Israel's distinctions and blessings.

For an Example to Men

But God has had and does have further purposes in Israel. He chose them to show all men His graciousness and long-suffering in dealing with sinful man. When God purposed to show the exceeding riches of His goodness to sinful man, He decided to do it on a national scale with Israel as the nation of His choice. I have heard, and no doubt you have also, many preachers who hold lengthy discourses on the disobedience and perverseness of Israel as God dealt with them throughout their early history and their later development. It seems never to have struck these preachers that God, desiring to show His longsuffering even with us of His children today, gave us a diagram of His ways and methods in His transactions with Israel. If I want to see how patient God is with me in my own life, which is marred from time to time with sin and disobedience, I have only to study the pages of God's Word to note how longsuffering He was with Israel. This is more wise, to be sure, and more in accordance with the purposes of God's plans (Romans 15:4) than to scan the pages of Israel's history to see how disobedient they were, in order to heap condemnation upon them.

Let us note some instances in which the character of God's dealings with Israel was manifest. When sinful man became estranged from the presence of the holy God through his own sin and disobedience, God provided in the Levitical offerings and ministrations an effective, though not a permanently adequate, way of approach to Himself. The longsuffering of God is all the more apparent when we remember that the blood of bulls and goats can never take away sin. It was because in the mind of God, the Lamb was slain from the foundation of the world, that He graciously accepted the Levitical offerings which He had commanded in His goodness. Surely this was grace upon grace.

How patient God can be with punishment-deserving sinners is further seen in the account of the wilderness wanderings. Sometimes it wears out our patience to read of these often repeated disobediences, but they never proved God to be anything but of long patience and infinitely kind. Just call these events to mind: the murmuring at Marah over the bitter water, the murmuring in the wilderness of Sin for some food like the fleshpots of Egypt, the striving at Rephidim for water, the worship of the golden calf at Sinai, the murmuring at Taberah, the stubbornness at Kibroth-hattaavah, the contention of Miriam and Aaron with Moses over his Cushite wife, the unbelieving report of ten of the spies who went into Canaan, the consequent rebellion of the people at Kadesh-barnea, their willfulness and defeat at Hormah, the rebellion of Korah, the murmuring of the people because of the death of Korah and his allies, the striving at the waters of Meribah, their complaint over the wilderness life while compassing the land of Edom in their journeying from Mount Hor, and the sin at Peor.

But as though these were not sufficient, the tale of sin in the time of the Judges completes the dismal picture of the early history of Israel from their Exodus from Egypt to their conquest and settlement of the land. The entire Book of Judges is one long contrast between what God commanded Israel under Moses and Joshua not to do, and what they did in spite of the warnings. It records step after step of their prolonged degradation.

The course of the history of the period is well summed up in these words:

"Then the sons of Israel did evil in the sight of the LORD, *and served the Baals, and they forsook the* LORD, *the God of their fathers, who had brought them out of the land of Egypt, and followed other gods from among the gods of the peoples who were around them, and bowed themselves down to them; thus they provoked the* LORD *to anger. So they forsook the* LORD *and served Baal and the Astartes. And the anger of the* LORD *burned against Israel, and He gave them into the hands of plunderers who plundered them; and He sold them into the hands of their enemies around them, so that they could no longer stand before their enemies. Wherever they went, the hand of the* LORD *was against them for evil, as the* LORD *had spoken and as the* LORD *had sworn to them, so that they were severely distressed.*

"Then the LORD *raised up judges who delivered them from the hands of those who plundered them. And yet they did not listen to their judges, for they played the harlot after other gods and bowed themselves down to them. They turned aside quickly from the way in which their fathers had walked in obeying the commandments of the* LORD; *they did not do as their fathers. And when the* LORD *raised up judges for them, the Lord was with the judge and delivered them... from those who oppressed and afflicted them. But it came about when the judge died, that they would turn back and act more corruptly than their fathers, in following other gods to serve them and bow down to them; they did not abandon their practices or their stubborn ways."*   (Judges 2:11-19)

What a commentary this is of the period of the Judges in Israel!

Later recorded history shows Israel departing time and time again from the Lord, and yet His patient faithfulness never failed. Malachi revealed the secret of it all: *"For I, the*

LORD, *do not change; therefore you, O sons of Jacob, are not consumed'"* (Malachi 3:6). And what shall we say of their subsequent refusal to accept their King Messiah? But are all these things revealed to show Israel more sinful than any other nation God has formed? A thousand times no. God was showing throughout how merciful and tender He can be to judgment-deserving sinners. Truly, Israel meant much to God in making this universal exhibit of His own long-suffering.

Yet there are still other ways in which Israel has meant and does mean much to God. When God in His sovereign counsel determined to reveal to the world the futility of works as a means of acceptance with Him, He chose Israel for the purpose. With reference to the history of Israel before they had come to Mt. Sinai, God had said: *"'You yourselves have seen what I did to the Egyptians, and how I bore you on eagles' wings, and brought you to Myself'"* (Exodus 19:4). Yet at the very first suggestion of the law, Israel as one man declared: *"'All that the LORD has spoken we will do'"* (Exodus 19:8). After all the commandments had been outlined, Israel said again: *"'All the words which the LORD has spoken we will do'"* (Exodus 24:3). What consummate confidence in and reliance upon the flesh this was. So from that time on, Israel has committed itself to the task of becoming justified before God by the deeds of the Law.

How they have succeeded, or rather failed, is revealed in Romans 9:30-10:4: *"What shall we say then? That Gentiles, who did not pursue righteousness, attained righteousness, even the righteousness which is by faith; but Israel, pursuing a law of righteousness, did not arrive at that law. Why? Because they did not pursue it by faith, but as though it were by works. . . . For I bear them witness that they have a zeal for God, but not in accordance with knowledge. For not knowing about God's righteousness, and seeking to establish their own, they did not subject themselves to the righteousness of God. For Christ is the end of the law for righteousness to everyone who believes."*

When the eternal and omniscient God wanted to prove experimentally and without a doubt before the world that by the works of the Law no flesh would be justified in His sight, in His great permissive will He allowed Israel to be the instrument of this demonstration. Surely no one after this should be in doubt as to whether works will really "work" or not. They do not accomplish the desired end in salvation. Yet what a pitiful picture we see in many evangelical Protestant churches today: men and women who have had God's truth that all is by faith, nevertheless feel called upon to aid God in His plan of salvation for them by adding a smattering of works. It is as though God were saying to them: "Do you not see that such a procedure will avail you nothing? Have I not demonstrated it on a national scale with My own people Israel and proved it to be a failure? Can you perform more works than they have outlined for themselves in the keeping of the Law?" What a lesson this is to teach a sinful world that loves to hide the sin nature behind a smoke screen of so-called "good works" and how necessary God found Israel for this purpose!

But God has used Israel, furthermore, to manifest His faithfulness to His promises. Many delight to think of the promise in Romans 11:29: *"For the gifts and the calling of God are irrevocable."* But they forget that this refers primarily to Israel, for the apostle decrees in the preceding verse: *"From the standpoint of the gospel they are enemies for your sake, but from the standpoint of God's choice they are beloved for the sake of the fathers."* In fact, the main design of the three chapters on Israel in the Epistle to the Romans, chapters 9, 10, and 11, is to show that, in spite of the fact that God has placed both Jew and Gentile in the same need of salvation and has placed salvation on a basis where it is free to both, yet God has abrogated none of His precious promises to Israel. If one is in doubt as to the reality of these promises, he needs only to begin with Genesis and will find them all along the way through the Old Testament, particularly in the prophecies of the prophetic books.

It seems, from my limited human standpoint, that God has ample ground for annulling every promise He has made to Israel because of their disobedience, but God is faithful to all His unconditional promises. With what confidence, then, is the child of God today to look to his heavenly Father in all that He has promised to His believing children. If God has kept and is keeping faith with Israel in all that has been promised them, then there need be no fear that God will fail to bring to blessed fruition all that He has ever spoken of regarding anyone. Israel, as it were, serves as a test case in the matter; since God has manifested His faithfulness with them, then He can be trusted by all.

For the Gospel and God's Glory

All these features that have been discussed thus far have been more or less with regard to the past of Israel's history. But the Word reveals that Israel will mean much to God in the future, when He uses them as worldwide missionaries. You have surely heard, as have I, that the world must be entirely evangelized in this age, and the task belongs to the Church. This view is prevalent even among many who do not hold that the whole world must be saved before Christ can return to the earth. Much of the error, if not the root of it, lies in a misinterpretation of Matthew 24:14: *"And this gospel of the kingdom shall be preached in the whole world for a witness to all the nations, and then the end shall come."*

This has consistently been applied to the Church by numbers of people. Such a wrong meaning of the verse can arise from but one thing: a failure to consider the context. The context reveals unmistakably that Israel is being spoken of. The time is the time of Jacob's trouble or the Great Tribulation. It is then that Israel will be God's Paul, multiplied thousands of times, to tell the story of the Gospel of the Kingdom to all the nations. These heralds are revealed in Revelation 7 as the 144,000 out of all the tribes of Israel. The result of their testimony is also set forth: the great unnumbered multitude from every kindred, tribe, tongue, and nation.

When God wants worldwide missionaries, He will again take up Israel. They will be a host of Jonahs back on their right jobs. Note it as a scriptural truth: whenever God wants things done on a national scale or desires a national testimony, He always chooses Israel. Then, do you not think that Israel means much to Him?

In the future God will yet employ Israel, His glory, to spread abroad the glory and knowledge of Himself in the Millennium. It is true that those who enter into the earthly kingdom of our Lord and Saviour will know Him, but a millennium is a long time. Scripture discloses that there will be birth and death then, so that there will arise generations of men who will need to be taught the knowledge of God. Israel has already been chosen for this important task.

Of the many Scriptures possible and available we note two. Isaiah 2:2-3 reads: *"In the last days, the mountain of the house of the* Lord *will be established as the chief of the mountains, and will be raised above the hills; and all the nations will stream to it. And many peoples will come and say, 'Come, let us go up to the mountain of the* Lord, *to the house of the God of Jacob; that He may teach us concerning His ways, and that we may walk in His paths.' For the law will go forth from Zion, and the word of the* Lord *from Jerusalem."* Zechariah 8:20-23 says this: *"'Thus says the* Lord *of hosts, "It will yet be that peoples will come, even the inhabitants of many cities; and the inhabitants of one will go to another saying, 'let us go at once to entreat the favor of the* Lord, *and to seek the* Lord *of hosts; I will also go.' So, many peoples and mighty nations will come to seek the* Lord *of hosts in Jerusalem and to entreat the favor of the* Lord." *Thus says the* Lord *of hosts, "In those days ten men from the nations of every language will grasp the garment of a Jew saying, 'Let us go with you, for we have heard that God is with you.'"'"* These Scripture passages tell a story that needs no comment.

To summarize, then, it has been shown that Israel means much to God, for He has purposed to use them to witness to the unity of His person; to show the blessedness of serving Him; to receive, preserve, and transmit the Scriptures; to show the sustaining power of the Scriptures throughout the centuries; to be the channel of the Messiah's incarnation; to show His longsuffering in dealing with sinful man; to reveal to the world the futility of seeking to gain acceptance with Him by works of the flesh; to manifest His faithfulness to His promises; to use them as worldwide missionaries; and to spread abroad the glory and knowledge of Himself in the Millennium. If God can so use them, do you not think they ought to mean a great deal to Him? The word to you and to me is clear: *"You who remind the* LORD, *take no rest for yourselves; and give Him no rest until He establishes and makes Jerusalem a praise in the earth"* (Isaiah 62:6-7).

15

The Crown Rights to David's Throne

THE VERY IMPORTANT QUESTION, "Who has the crown rights to David's throne?" has recently come to the fore with a great deal of interest. A practicing dentist in Jerusalem has founded a Royalist Party with a membership of 150 Israeli citizens. He has appointed himself "regent" of his eight-year-old son whom he expects to proclaim as king of Israel. The second candidate for the Davidic throne, a certain employee of the Palestine Foundation Fund, considers himself a direct descendant of King David and threatens to sue his competitor in the Supreme Court of Israel for falsely claiming Israel's throne. Who has the right in this matter?

THE THRONE

The classic passage is found in 2 Samuel 7:10-16, which reads: "*'I will also appoint a place for My people Israel and will plant them, that they may live in their own place and not be disturbed again; nor will the wicked afflict them any more as formerly, even from the day that I commanded judges to be over My people Israel; and I will give you rest from all your enemies. The LORD also declares to you that the LORD will make a house for you. When your days are complete and you lie down with your fathers, I will raise up your descendant after you, who will come forth from you, and I will establish his kingdom. He shall build a house for My name, and I will establish the throne of his kingdom forever. I will be a father to him and he will be a son to Me; when he commits iniquity, I will correct him with the rod of men and the strokes of the sons of men, but My lovingkindness shall not depart from him, as I took it away from Saul, whom I removed from before you. And your house and your kingdom shall endure before Me forever; your throne shall be established forever.'"*

Every word of the covenant or contract is vital. Three outstanding features mark the covenant. First of all, it is promised of God. No human agency thought out this particular plan and no human hand instituted it. God was the moving Personality here.

Second, the throne is an unconditional gift. Nowhere in the wording of the promise is there a condition attached to the establishment of Davidic sovereignty or the Davidic throne. There is a warning that sin in David's line would be visited with punishment, but it would not impair the throne rights to David and his descendants. Third, it is eternal in duration. All human thrones are for a time. They arise in time and will pass in the course of time. This throne alone is of eternal duration. It will have no end; it will go on into eternity.

THE OCCUPANT

It is readily understood that David's descendants became more numerous as the generations passed. To which one of them did the throne rights belong?

The credentials of the rightful heir are clearly set forth. His birthplace is indicted in Micah 5:2: *"'But as for you, Bethlehem Ephrathah, too little to be among the clans of Judah, from you One will go forth for Me to be ruler in Israel. His goings forth are from long ago, from the days of eternity.'"*

The time of the birth of the King is noted in Daniel 9:24-27:

"Seventy weeks have been decreed for your people and your holy city, to finish the transgression, to make an end of sin, to make atonement for iniquity, to bring in everlasting righteousness, to seal up vision and prophecy, and to anoint the most holy place. So you are to know and discern that from the issuing of a decree to restore and rebuild Jerusalem until Messiah the Prince there will be seven weeks and sixty-two weeks; it will be built again, with plaza and moat, even in times of distress. Then after the sixty-two weeks the Messiah will be cut off and have nothing, and the people of the prince who is to come will destroy the city and the sanctuary. And its end will come with a flood; even to the end there will be war; desolations are determined. And he will make a firm covenant with the many for one week, but in the middle of the week he will put a stop to sacrifice and grain offering; and on the wing of abominations will come one who makes desolate, even until a complete destruction, one that is decreed, is poured out on the one who makes desolate."

The manner of His birth is stated in Isaiah 7:14: *"'Therefore the Lord Himself will give you a sign: Behold, a virgin will be with child and bear a son, and she will call His name Immanuel.'"* And His nature is described in Isaiah 9:6-7: *"For a child will be born to us, a son will be given to us; and the government will rest on His shoulders; and His name will be called Wonderful Counselor, Mighty God, Eternal Father, Prince of Peace. There will be no end to the increase of His government or of peace, on the throne of David and over his kingdom, to establish it and to uphold it with justice and righteousness from then on and forevermore. The zeal of the* LORD *of hosts will accomplish this.'"* He was to be both human and divine.

It is told of Roman Emperor Theodosius that he denied the deity of Christ. When his son Arcadius was about sixteen he decided to make him a partner with himself in the government of the empire. Among the great men who assembled themselves to congratulate the new wearer of the imperial purple was a bishop by the name of Amphilocus. He made a splendid and eloquent address to the emperor and was ready to leave when Theodosius exclaimed: "What! Do you take no notice of my son?"

Then the bishop went up to Arcadius and putting his hands upon his head said: "The Lord bless thee, my son!"

The emperor, aroused to fury by this slight to his son, exclaimed, "What! Is this all the reverence you pay to one whom I have determined to make of equal dignity and honor with myself?"

Amphilocus answered: "Sire, you do very highly resent my apparent neglect of your son, because I do not give him equal honors with yourself. Then, what must the Eternal God think of you when you degrade His co-equal and co-eternal Son to the level of one of His creatures?" The emperor realized that the reproof was just and deserved.

THE DOUBLE CLAIM

He who would have David's throne must present a double claim to it. This fact has been overlooked by the present contestants for the throne and by the majority in Israel. The King is no ordinary king. The King must be a Priest also. Psalm 110:1-4 reads: *"The LORD says to my Lord: 'Sit at My right hand, until I make Thine enemies a footstool for Thy feet.' The LORD will stretch forth Thy strong scepter from Zion, saying, 'Rule in the midst of Thine enemies.' Thy people will volunteer freely in the day of Thy power; in holy array, from the womb of the dawn, Thy youth are to Thee as the dew. The LORD has sworn and will not change His mind, 'Thou art a priest forever according to the order of Melchizedek.'"* Zechariah 6:12-13 indicates: *"'Then say to him, "Thus says the LORD of hosts, 'Behold, a man whose name is Branch, for He will branch out from where He is; and He will build the*

temple of the LORD. *Yes, it is He who will build the temple of
the* LORD, *and He who will bear the honor and sit and rule on
His throne. Thus, He will be a priest on His throne, and the
counsel of peace will be between the two offices.'"'"* He must
make redemption from sin before He can rule. Only One can
ever qualify here and it is the Lord Jesus Christ, the Messiah
of Israel. Notice how soon in the gospel His royal descent
(Matthew 1:1) is linked with His priestly work (Matthew
1:21).

A woman in India had learned that she was a sinner and in
a lost estate. She had been told from the Word of God that
God is holy and cannot overlook sin. She often said, "I need
some great prince or ruler to stand between my soul and
God." After some time she heard that the Bible itself contained the account of a Saviour who had died for sinners. So
she asked a Pundit, a learned scholar of India, to read the
Bible to her. He began at the first chapter of Matthew, and as
he read the list of names in the genealogy of Christ, the
woman thought, "What a wonderful prince this Jesus must be
to have such a long line of eminent ancestors." And when the
Pundit read, "Thou shalt call his name Jesus; for he shall save
his people from their sins," the woman exclaimed with joy,
"Ah, this is the Prince I want! The Prince who is also a
Saviour!"

Such is the one you need and I need. We need the royal
descendant of David who is a Saviour. No man can lay claim
to this except the Messiah of Israel, the Lord Jesus. He must
be trusted alone as Saviour and recognized as King.

16

Why the Jews do not Believe
in Christ

WE DO NOT IMPLY that no Jews believe in the Lord Jesus Christ as Saviour and Messiah. From the beginning of our Lord's ministry He had Jewish followers. Note John 1:41: *"He found first his own brother Simon, and said to him, 'We have found the Messiah' (which translated means Christ)."* At Pentecost the great ingathering was from the Jews. Acts 2:5 mentions explicitly *"Jews..., devout men."* Every succeeding century has seen Jews devoted to the Lord Jesus Christ as Redeemer, and this day is no exception. But manifestly there are many Jews who do not believe in Christ. In fact, the majority come under this category. Let us be reminded that this is true of every other nation under heaven. But with Israel we expect it to be different because the Christian faith began in their midst and is rooted in the Old Testament Scriptures. Why, then, do the Jews as such not believe in Christ? The reasons are several and the situation is a complex one.

PREJUDICE

Prejudice is an unreasonable objection against anything or any person, an opinion against anything without just grounds or before sufficient knowledge. Many Jews do not believe in Christ because they are prejudiced against Him and the Gospel. They know that their parents, friends, and their leaders do not follow the Christian faith, so they do not have any desire to do so. The passage in John 7:45-48 is in point here: *"The officers therefore came to the chief priests and Pharisees, and they said to them, 'Why did you not bring Him?' The officers answered, 'Never did a man speak the way this man speaks.' The Pharisees therefore answered them, 'You have not also been led astray, have you? No one of the rulers or Pharisees has believed in Him, has he?'"* They have often heard derogatory remarks about Christ and have accepted these pronouncements without question. Often they have not taken the time to investigate the question of the claims of Christ at all. In this they are like many unbelieving Gentiles. Also, the Christian faith with its distinctive theology, worship, and outlook is strange to the Jew. Men easily form prejudices against that which is strange to them. Prejudices die hard.

When Galileo was summoned before the inquisition to be tried for the "heresy" of declaring the revolution of the earth, he said to his judges: "I can convince you. Here is my telescope; look through it and you will see the moons of Jupiter." They refused to look. They were convinced that the earth did not revolve around the sun, and no amount of evidence could persuade them otherwise!

BLINDNESS

Many Jews do not believe in Christ because they cannot honestly see in Him the Messiah of Israel. They are blind spiritually. Romans 11:25 says, *"For I do not want you, brethren, to be uninformed of this mystery, lest you be wise in your own estimation, that a partial hardening has happened to Israel until the fulness of the Gentiles has come in."* We read further in 2 Corinthians 3:12-16: *"Having therefore such a hope, we use great boldness in our speech, and are not as Moses, who used to put a veil over his face that the sons of Israel might not look intently at the end of what was fading away. But their minds were hardened; for until this very day at the reading of the old covenant the same veil remains unlifted, because it is removed in Christ. But to this day whenever Moses is read, a veil lies over their heart; but whenever a man turns to the Lord, the veil is taken away."*

There is a blindness upon the Gentiles also, as indicated in Isaiah 25:7 and 2 Corinthians 3:3-4. Thus, when the Gospel is explained and given to the Jew, there must be earnest prayer that the blindness may be removed from his eyes. We do not help blind men by placing stumbling blocks in their way. When the Jewish heart turns to the Lord, the blindness of the Jewish heart is removed.

A minister was preaching on Glasgow Green once when someone asked permission to speak, and made his way to the platform. "Friends," he said, "I do not believe what this man has been talking about. I do not believe in a hell, in a judgment, in a God, for I never saw any of them."

He continued talking in this way for a while, when another voice was heard from the crowd. "May I speak?" The infidel sat down, and the next man began.

"Friends, you say there is a river running not far from this place, the river Clyde. There is no such thing; it is not true. You tell me that there are grass and trees growing around me where I now stand; there is no such thing; that also is untrue. You tell me that there are a great many people standing here. Again, I say that is not true; there is no person standing here except myself. I suppose you wonder what I am talking about; but friends, I was born blind. I never have seen any of you, and while I talk it only shows I am blind or I would not say such things. And you," he said, turning to the infidel, "the more you talk the more it exposes your own ignorance, because you are spiritually blind, and cannot see. Dear friends, by faith ye are saved. In Christ you will find life and love and everlasting joy."

PERSECUTION

The persecution of Jews by so-called Christians through the centuries cannot be easily erased from the memory. It is vivid in the thinking of the Jews of every generation and especially of this generation. An aged Jew is credited with having said: "He cannot be our Messiah whose followers persecute us so." And the day has passed when we can blame it all on the Roman Catholic Church, Hitler, or the Greek Orthodox Church. There are those in fundamental circles who are viciously spreading abroad anti-Semitic propaganda and falsehoods. You can imagine to what extent this can go when such a leader held that Jesus was not a Jew.

Some Jews (if not many), too, know they will not be welcome in the churches. Prominent Christian leaders and educators of ministers write concerning the commercialism of Christmas. When they do they indicate that the entire country is in the grasp of a great commercial movement, and are careful to say that it is in large part in the hands of Jewish merchants who in their hearts hate the name of Jesus. But they are not averse to using His coming into the world to promote an upsurge of commercial activities. We ought to know that it was no Jew in our land who promoted such efforts by meddling with the holiday calendar. For all persecutions of the Jews, of whatever kind, God will hold the perpetrators responsible.

IGNORANCE

Some may be surprised to know that many Jews do not believe in Christ because they have never heard the Gospel. True, they may have taken the blessed name of Christ in an oath or heard others do so, but how many have truly heard the simple, clear story of the Gospel's redeeming grace? Comparatively few. How could they know when they do not go to church, have never been witnessed to, and do not realize the message is intended for them also? Too often we hear the statement "Christianity is for the Gentiles." Jews should be told and told again and retold that the Gospel and salvation in Jesus the Messiah is for them and they must have it. The words of Romans 10:13-15 are still applicable: *"For, 'Who-*

ever will call upon the name of the Lord will be saved.' How then shall they call upon Him in whom they have not believed? And how shall they believe in Him whom they have not heard? And how shall they hear without a preacher? And how shall they preach unless they are sent? Just as it is written, 'How beautiful are the feet of those who bring glad tidings of good things!'"

May God stir our hearts to give Israel the Gospel in these dark days. Time is short and the opportunity will not be ours forever. We must do it now!

17

Will a Retrial of Jesus
Take Place?

UNDOUBTEDLY the trial of Jesus the Messiah of Israel is the most celebrated trial in the history of the world. More investigation and more books have been devoted to it than to any other. Every new generation restudies it and makes its pronouncement upon it. With the recent rebirth of the political State of Israel in the Holy Land, the question has taken on added interest in some quarters. The question has arisen and is to the fore, Will they retry Jesus of Nazareth?

To put the whole question in the proper light, we must keep in mind these facts: the trial itself, the attempts at retrial, and the impossibility of a retrial.

THE TRIAL ITSELF

The passages in the Scripture that treat the trial itself in the life of Christ are found in all four gospels: Matthew 26:57-75; Mark 14:53-65; Luke 22:54-71; John 18:13-18, 24-27. The steps in the trial were these:

First, He was brought privately before Annas, the father-in-law of Caiaphas. The record reads: *"So the Roman cohort and the commander, and the officers of the Jews, arrested Jesus and bound Him, and led Him to Annas first; for he was father-in-law of Caiaphas, who was high priest that year. Now Caiaphas was the one who had advised the Jews that it*

was expedient for one man to die on behalf of the people"
(John 18:12-14).

Second, He was questioned by Annas. The substance of this interview is given to us also. *"The high priest therefore questioned Jesus about His disciples, and about His teaching. Jesus answered him, 'I have spoken openly to the world; I always taught in synagogues, and in the temple, where all the Jews come together; and I spoke nothing in secret. Why do you question Me? Question those who have heard what I spoke to them; behold, these know what I said.' And when He had said this, one of the officers standing by gave Jesus a blow, saying, 'Is that the way you answer the high priest?' Jesus answered him, 'If I have spoken wrongly, bear witness of the wrong; but if rightly, why do you strike Me?'"* This was strictly an unofficial interview (John 18:19-23).

Third, He was sent by Annas to Caiaphas. We read: *"Annas therefore sent Him bound to Caiaphas the high priest"* (John 18:24). This was for the formal trial before the proper court.

Fourth, He was tried judicially and condemned by the Sanhedrin. The record is clear: *"Now the chief priests and the whole Council kept trying to obtain testimony against Jesus to put Him to death; and they were finding none. For many were giving false testimony against Him, and yet their testimony was not consistent. And some stood up and began to give false testimony against Him, saying, 'We heard Him say, "I will destroy this temple made with hands, and in three days I will build another made without hands."' And not even in this respect was their testimony consistent. And the high priest arose and came forward and questioned Jesus, saying, 'Do you make no answer to what these men are testifying against you?' But He kept silent and made no answer. Again the high priest was questioning Him, and saying to Him, 'Are You the Christ, the Son of the Blessed One?' And Jesus said, 'I am; and you shall see the Son of Man sitting at the right hand of Power, and coming with the clouds of heaven.' And tearing his clothes, the high priest said, 'What further need do we have of witnesses? You have heard the blasphemy; how does it seem to you?' And they all condemned Him to be deserving of death"* (Mark 14:55-64). He was condemned to death on the charge of blasphemy. The Mosaic Law had stipulated death by stoning for anyone who committed the sin of blasphemy (Leviticus 24:16).

Last, He was shamefully treated. This wholly unbecoming action is described thus: *"And some began to spit at Him, and to blindfold Him, and to beat Him with their fists, and to say to Him 'Prophesy!' And the officers received Him with slaps in the face."* (Mark 14:65).

The irregularities in the procedure of the trial have been pointed out again and again. But in such discussions we must not forget that all this was foretold in the Old Testament. He was to be falsely accused (Psalm 35:11). He was to be maltreated, spit upon, and the hair of His beard was to be plucked (Isaiah 50:6). Unresisting, He was to be beaten (Isaiah 50:6; 53:5). He was condemned and oppressed, as well as mercilessly treated (Isaiah 53:7-9). These same passages indicate that He was tried for no fault in Him but for our sakes, Israel's, and the world's. Christ was on trial for us. The Messiah of Israel was brought into judgment for each one of us.

Dr. Bainbridge some years ago reached Tokyo, Japan, on a missionary journey. He expected to remain there for some time. One morning an official asked him this question: "Who stands for you?" Thinking that he was speaking of passports, he showed his, but that was not what was wanted. He then offered letters of introduction that he had, but they too were unsatisfactory, and the question was repeated, "Who stands for you?" It was explained that there was a law in that city that no foreigner could take up his residence there for any length of time unless he provided himself with a "substitute." He found there were nationals who hired themselves out to foreigners for this purpose. If the foreigner violated any law, the substitute suffered the penalty for him. If the penalty should be death, the substitute suffered the penalty of death.

Dr. Bainbridge secured a substitute and was allowed to remain in peace. Such a substitute was Christ for us at the trial; the Messiah took our place and suffered the penalty of death for us who had transgressed the Law of God.

In this matter of the retrial of Jesus, we must consider, in the second place, the attempts at retrial.

THE ATTEMPTS AT RETRIAL

There have been those who have advocated a retrial of Jesus on the ground that the original trial was a miscarriage of justice. Better than a dozen years ago a Jewish attorney in this country proposed such a retrial. Much publicity was given it, but nothing came of it when the attorney himself committed suicide.

Not long after the establishment of the State of Israel, the newly constituted Supreme Court of the land had a petition filed with it for a retrial of Jesus. The petitioner was a Dutch Protestant by the name of Henri Groskamp. During the German occupation of Holland in World War II, he read much on the trial of Jesus of Nazareth while he was in hiding from the Nazis. In the summer of 1948 he appealed to the World Council of Churches in Amsterdam. Now he had a legally drawn-up brief before the Supreme Court of Israel. He argued: (1) Caiaphas violated accepted Jewish legal procedure in the trial. (2) Jesus was rejected because He was no national liberator. But Israel's rebirth now without a Messiah proves that Israel's Messiah did not have to be a national deliverer. On this latter point Groskamp had not fully considered the prophecies of the Old Testament, nor such a New Testament word as: *"Salvation from our enemies, and from the hand of all who hate us"* (Luke 1:71).

Supreme Court President Justice Moshe Smoira said the petition brings up an interesting question. "The action we will take," he said, "turns on the question of jurisdiction—whether our court can be considered a successor court to the

Sanhedrin or can go into a purely religious question." Legal and religious experts are sure the Supreme Court of Israel will ultimately drop the case for lack of jurisdiction, or right to speak in the matter. The case has not been heard of.

Since 1948 there have been no open petitions for a retrial, but a large and growing literature on the subject is coming from diverse sources, Jewish and Gentile. Widely discussed and debated has been the work of S. G. F. Brandon of the University of Manchester on *The Trial of Jesus of Nazareth* (1968). Jesus is portrayed as sympathetic to the Zealot movement with its political overtones. Much of the argument is based on incidental references, like Christ's statement regarding the sword (compare the Sicarri, swordbearers and Zealots). It is doubtful that this kind of approach will have any lasting effect.

In 1967 Haim H. Cohn, Justice of the Supreme Court of Israel, published his noted work entitled *Reflectións on the Trial and Death of Jesus*. Justice Cohn is an expert in Jewish legal traditions. He contends that not only did the Jews have no part in the trial of Christ, but that the Sanhedrin tried to save Him from death. He suggested that the Sanhedrin was eager to find men to testify in favor of Jesus, and was trying to persuade Jesus to enter a not guilty plea before the Roman authorities. The thesis appeared in the *Israel Law Review*. He claims Jesus was tried and condemned for the political crime of insurrection, a charge that could be adjudicated only by the Roman procurator, not by a Jewish court. He based the argument on Pilate's question: "Are you King of the Jews?" and Jesus' answer: "You have said so," a declaration tantamount, according to Cohn, to a nolo contendere admission of guilt. Without going into the ramifications of the subject, which are vastly important, it must be stated that Justice Cohn's position makes a shambles of the Gospel evidence of the trial proceedings, leaving far too much unexplained and injecting insufferable confusion into the whole matter. Furthermore, Jesus' answer to Pilate can never be construed as Cohn has it, for this violates a well-known Greek idiom, which is a strong asseveration. The learned jurist has read his own interpretation into the statement.[1]

But we must recognize at once that, in the last analysis, there is the impossibility of a retrial.

THE IMPOSSIBILITY OF A RETRIAL

When once the question of a retrial is thought through in its many details, it can be seen that a retrial of Jesus is impossible.

1. If it were attempted, it would be a farce and valueless. There is no body nor council now with the authority and jurisdiction of the Sanhedrin. World Jewry has no single body that can adjudicate for it in religious matters. There is no voice that will be universally heeded among them. The powers which were exercised by the old Sanhedrin are not found to reside in any similar body or group today.

2. It is impossible to bring Christ personally to trial now, as they did then. He is at the right hand of the Father according to Psalm 110:1 and Hebrews 2:9. They cannot bring Him down from thence. Unbelievers claim He is no longer living, and that His body has gone into dissolution like all dead bodies. If this vicious lie were true, then it still points up the fact that Jesus can no longer be brought back visibly and personally to stand trial. An empty decision either way on the question may satisfy some minds on the legal level, but what would it accomplish in actuality? The world has not seen Him (though His disciples did) since His resurrection, and it will not see Him again until He comes to judge the earth in righteousness (Psalm 98:9).

3. No judicial or religious body can now reverse the results of the death sentence. The penalty has been paid to the full. Who has the power to reverse this fact?

4. No Scripture even intimates that He will be retried.

The most solemn feature of the whole question is that spiritually Christ is still on trial before the bar and court of

---

[1] *Time*, 10 November 1967, p. 76.

every unbelieving heart. You must answer: "What then shall I do with Jesus who is called the Christ?" And it is boundless and eternal tragedy to condemn Him in the court of your heart. He was condemned to death once to purchase your salvation and mine. It was a tremendous price, but He paid it.

In Arizona an Indian boy was plowing corn. His little sister was playing behind a mud hut among the stones. On this great desert there were many rattlesnakes. The little girl turned over a stone, and there was a great rattlesnake. It coiled and struck her deep in the flesh of the leg. She screamed aloud; her brother heard in the field and rushed to her aid. Seeing at once what had happened, he killed the snake with the heel of his boot, then took his sister in his arms and, holding his two hands tightly about the wound, placed his lips to it, sucked out the deadly poison, and spit it out on the ground. He had saved her life, but he lost his own for he had a sore in his mouth which the poison entered. The Lord Jesus Christ, God's Son, when we all had been bitten by the old serpent, heard the cry of need. He came down to us from heaven, dealt a blow to the "old serpent, the Devil" and took the sin poison from us. And it was our sin that caused His death.

18

Is Jewish Evangelism
God's Stepchild?

A STEPCHILD according to the dictionary "is a child by one's wife or husband by a former marriage." It is also used in the sense of "anything likened to a stepchild, especially as not receiving solicitous attention." Can Jewish evangelism, then, be likened to a stepchild as far as God and His program are concerned? Have efforts for the salvation of the lost in Israel come in for undeservedly scant attention from many of the children of God? Is this the will of God concerning Israel? We ask the question in all seriousness and directness, "Is Jewish evangelism God's stepchild?"

To find its adequate answer, we consider first the question in light of the purpose and preparation of the Gospel.

IN THE PURPOSE AND PREPARATION OF THE GOSPEL

Are we to answer the question from the purpose of the gospel? If we wish to find out whether God left Israel out of the picture, let us hear the words of the blessed Messiah Himself (Matthew 23:37): *"O Jerusalem, Jerusalem, who kills the prophets and stones those who are sent to her! How often I wanted to gather your children together, the way a hen gathers her chicks under her wings, and you were unwilling."* We cannot misjudge these words of our Lord or fail properly to interpret them.

When the great apostle Paul declared the truth of the Gospel, he said in Romans 1:16: *"For I am not ashamed of the gospel, for it is the power of God for salvation to everyone who believes, to the Jew first and also to the Greek."* Did he mean to overlook the lost in Israel? Were Jews included or excluded here? Is it even indicated that they were to take a secondary place?

No, they were to have the Gospel as well as other nations, and in the matter of order they were to have it proclaimed to them first of all.

In Matthew 2:2 the wise men that came from the East did not think that Israel was a secondary issue in the program of redemption. John the Baptist did not think so (Matthew 3:1). The Messiah never intimated that He thought the salvation of Israel was a minor or unessential matter (Matthew 4:14-17). Hear these clear words: *"These twelve Jesus sent out after instructing them, saying, 'Do not go in the way of the Gentiles, and do not enter any city of the Samaritans; but rather go to the lost sheep of the house of Israel'"* (Matthew 10:5-7).

When the disciples of the Messiah went out preaching in the cities of Judea, they did not think Jewish evangelism was of no consequence. The seventy (Luke 10:1, 17) felt Israel was central in the purpose of God concerning the Gospel.

Nothing so perfectly reveals Horace T. Pitkin, who was killed in the Boxer Rebellion in China in 1900, as his last recorded words, spoken to his Chinese helper while the enraged crowd was swooping down upon the mission: "Laoman, tell the mother of little Horace that his father's last wish was that, when he is twenty-five years of age, he should come to China as a missionary."

Thus would God and the Messiah have us to go to the lost sheep of the house of Israel.

If we would find out whether Jewish evangelism is God's stepchild, we must, in the second place, think on the subject of the propagation of the Gospel.

IN THE PROPAGATION OF THE GOSPEL

Acts 1:8 records the words of the Lord Jesus the Messiah: *"But you shall receive power when the Holy Spirit has come upon you; and you shall be My witnesses both in Jerusalem, and in all Judaea and Samaria, and even to the remotest part of the earth."* This directive gives the Messiah's blueprint with the wisdom of high heaven for all the centuries of Christian testimony. It has never been altered, revoked, nor nullified. Read it in Acts 2:1-11, 22, 37-38; 3:1, 11-21; (Paul's ministry) Acts 9:15, 20, 28, 29; 13:5, 14 ff., 44-46; 14:1-7; 16:13; 17:1-5, 10, 16, 17; 18:1-6; and many others equally as plain, down to the end of the book of Acts.

In the third place, we must review Jewish evangelism in the program of the Church's missionary efforts.

IN THE PROGRAM OF THE CHURCH'S MISSIONARY EFFORTS

It has been well said: " 'To the Jew first,' reveals the divine strategy of missions, not only in the first century but in all centuries.... The Jew is the key of the world's missionary campaign." A German writer said, "In unbelief, as in belief, the Jews are the leaders of mankind." No other missionary effort or endeavor is more urgent than this. Professor Franz Delitzsch, the great Hebrew scholar, said, "For the Church to evangelize the world without thinking of the Jews, is like a bird trying to fly with one wing broken."

If we study the history of the Church we shall find that efforts to evangelize the Jews practically ceased about the time of the Emperor Constantine the Great, and soon the Church entered into the Dark Ages, a thousand years of spiritual darkness. The result was that the corrupt Church shifted from her true position and tried to set up a kingdom in a world setting with the religious leader reigning as the representative of Christ on earth. That was a costly mistake from which we have never recovered! For hundreds of years little or no attempt has been made to reach the needy Jew definitely with the Gospel of his Messiah and Saviour.

Conditions have changed somewhat today, but what room there is for improvement! How many churches have the evangelization of the Jew in their missionary budgets? How many of those who support hundreds of missionaries give the cause of Israel's salvation its rightful and scriptural place? How many Jewish missionaries are allowed into church groups to plead the cause of Jewish evangelization?

Rabinowitz, the noted Jewish-Christian lawyer of Russia, came to America for a visit in 1893, and then wrote: "The thirty-five days I spent in America were very sad and bitter days to me.... There I saw the sheep wandering through all the mountains and upon every high hill—yea, they are scattered upon all the face of the earth and none did search or seek after them! (Ezekiel 34:6). Oh, Jesus, my Saviour and King! Where are Thy messengers? Where are Thy preachers? Command them to come and save the lost ones in America!"

Are we to say Jewish evangelism is God's stepchild? It is only true if we judge from the bitter persecutions of the Jews, the millions of Jews dying in Christian lands without the Messiah, the multitudes in our land untouched by the message of the Gospel of redeeming and keeping grace, and the very little missionary work which is being done among the Jews. We act as though they were God's stepchildren, by our hate, indifference, or monopoly.

Finally, we cannot conclude the consideration of this significant theme until we are prepared to face the matter of Jewish evangelism.

IN ITS PRODUCTS AND RESULTS

Judging from the fruitage of this work, is it God's stepchild, His second-rate interest? No, a thousand times. In the last century 72,000 Jews accepted Jesus as Messiah and submitted to Protestant baptism, not to mention the 132,000 baptized into the Greek and Roman Churches. This made one Protestant convert to every 156 of the Jewish population. The number of baptized converts among the heathen and

Muslims in the same time was two million, or one to every 525 of the heathen and Muslim population. The same degree of success among the heathen and Muslims, as was realized among the Jews, would have shown seven million converts, instead of two million. Three times as many Jewish converts enter the Gospel ministry as of converts from among other nations. This field is most fruitful and blessed of God Himself. It is not God's stepchild, if we are to judge from the way He has blessed the efforts put forth.

Some years ago a clergyman of the Church of England had attended an early morning prayer meeting in behalf of Israel, in one of the East London Jewish missions. Coming out on the street he met a brother clergyman who had attended a special service at St. Paul's Cathedral on the anniversary of the conversion of St. Paul.

After greeting each other, the minister from St. Paul's service asked the other where he had been that morning. He told him he had attended a Jewish mission meeting, upon which the other showed some surprise that his friend should believe in the possibility of Jews being converted. The other asked him where he had been, and he told him that he had attended a special service in the cathedral that morning. "Who was St. Paul?" asked he. The hesitating reply was, "I suppose you would consider him a converted Jew." "What music did they have?" "Why Mendelssohn's 'St. Paul,' of course." "Who was Mendelssohn?" "Why a German." "No, he was not, he was a converted Jew," was the answer. "Who was the preacher?" "Dr. Jacobs, Bishop of St. Albans."

This man did not believe in converted Jews, and yet he had been in a church dedicated to the memory of a converted Jew; he had attended a service in honor of this Jew's conversion; he had listened to music composed by a converted Jew; he had heard a sermon preached by a converted Jew and was greeted by a converted Jew, for the other clergyman was the Reverend Mr. Aaron Bernstein, a converted Jew.

No one is so blind as he who will not see. It is as plain as the noonday sun that God has incorporated Israel in His pur-

poses of redemption through the death of the Messiah, the
Lord Jesus Christ. Their evangelization is not God's step-
child. But is it yours? Is it an immaterial matter to you? May
God reveal it to you otherwise as you prayerfully meditate on
His Word.

Jewish friend, uncounted is the number of those who have
through the centuries received the Messiah in Israel, to the
saving of their souls and their obtaining eternal life. They
have found that the salvation of Jewish souls is not irrelevant
or immaterial to God. They have found it central and have re-
joiced to make it known to their brethren according to the
flesh. The earnest entreaty this hour to your heart from a
believer in Israel, is "Believe on the Lord Jesus the Messiah,
and thou shalt be saved."

19

Do Jews Really Need to Be Saved?

THERE ARE THOSE who claim Israel have had their chance and now that is over. They have sinned away their opportunity and day of grace by their unbelief. They are prepared to say that the Jews as a whole cannot and will not be saved. Strangely enough, they who propose this view do not cite Scripture for this position. The reason is obvious: there is not one single particle of Scripture truth to be found in such an outlandish claim.

Then there are those who have surrounded the Jew with a certain halo and feel he does not need to be saved because he is of God's ancient people. He has, as it were, a charmed life and a special dispensation or distribution of God's grace allotted to him. This view is identical with the Jewish doctrine to be found in one of their prayers: "There is a portion for all Israel in the world to come." No Bible proof can be given for this position either. It is a matter of personal opinion or tradition of men.

Still others feel the Jews do not need to be saved now, because all Israel of all ages will be saved in the future. They point to the passage in Romans 11:25-27 which reads: *"For I do not want you, brethren, to be uninformed of this mystery, lest you be wise in your own estimation, that a partial hardening has happened to Israel until the fulness of the Gentiles has come in; and thus all Israel will be saved; just as it is written, 'The Deliverer will come from Zion, He will remove ungodli-*

217

ness from Jacob. And this is my covenant with them, When I take away their sins.'"

Those who advocate this view forget that there is no assurance that individual Jews will be living at that time who are on earth at this time. How do we know that individuals now living will continue to that hour? The Bible never places the acceptance of the Messiah by faith and the reception of His salvation, as a future decision. It always presents the matter of decision in the present. Moreover, we cannot fail to take into account the Scripture statement that there will be many unworthy in Israel who will come into judgment, just as the Gentiles will (Ezekiel 20:33-38). In short, the Scriptures do not support this view any more than the others. The question still remains and demands a clear answer: Do Jews really need to be saved?

Jews really and desperately need to be saved because, in the first place, the Bible reveals the universality of sin and condemnation.

The Universality of Sin and Condemnation

The Jew as well as the Gentile is under sin and the curse of God. Under what condemnation does the Jew rest? The apostle Paul answers in these words (Romans 2:17-24): *"But if you bear the name 'Jew,' and rely upon the Law, and boast in God, and know His will, and approve the things that are essential, being instructed out of the Law, and are confident that you yourself are a guide to the blind, a light to those who are in darkness, a corrector of the foolish, a teacher of the immature, having in the Law the embodiment of knowledge and of the truth, you, therefore, who teach another, do you not teach yourself? You who preach that one should not steal, do you steal? You who say that one should not commit adultery, do you commit adultery? You who abhor idols, do you rob temples? You who boast in the Law, through your breaking the Law, do you dishonor God? For 'the name of*

God is blasphemed among the Gentiles because of you,' just as it is written."

Did the apostle mean to imply by this very forceful passage that the Jew was in greater need of salvation than the Gentile? Hear him set forth the bill of particulars: (Romans 3:9-18): *"What then? Are we better than they? Not at all; for we have already charged that both Jews and Greeks are all under sin; as it is written, 'There is none righteous, not even one; there is none who understands, there is none who seeks for God; all have turned aside, together they have become useless; there is none who does good, there is not even one. Their throat is an open grave, with their tongues they keep deceiving, the poison of asps is under their lips; whose mouth is full of cursing and bitterness; their feet are swift to shed blood, destruction and misery are in their paths, and the path of peace have they not known. There is no fear of God before their eyes.'"*

This is an all-inclusive indictment which includes every Jew and Gentile on the face of the earth. The Jew is a sinner by nature and by practice, for all have actually sinned and come short of the glory of God (Romans 3:23). You may seek to deny it, but it is nonetheless still true, tragically so. Ephesians 2:1-3 concludes: *"Even as the rest."* The Law is unable to help, because it can only condemn the violater and is powerless to justify him (Romans 3:19-20; Galatians 3:21-22). There is need for God's righteousness. It will not do to be busy manufacturing your own. It cannot be recognized as acceptable in the sight of the thrice holy God (Romans 10:1-4). All in Israel are lost without the Messiah, the Lord Jesus Christ. What an urgency this places upon us and our message!

When the Duke of Kent, the father of Queen Victoria of England, lay dying, his physician tried to soothe his mind by referring to the distinguished position in which God had placed him. His quick and correct reply was: "Remember, if I am to be saved, it is not as a prince, but as a sinner." Christ came to call, not the righteous, but *all* sinners to repentance.

Every Jew in the world today needs to be redeemed and made fit for eternal life in heaven, because, in the second place, the Scriptures teach the impartiality of God's grace and salvation.

THE IMPARTIALITY OF GOD'S GRACE AND SALVATION

The remedy is specifically the same for all suffering from the same disease of sin. Both Jew and Gentile must be declared righteous in God's sight by the same medium and channel of faith (Romans 3:29-30). God's grace, His unmerited favor, is provided for both. He is rich toward both, and the same enablement is provided for them alike (Romans 10:12-13; Ephesians 2:18). That grace which has saved both Jews (Acts 2) and Gentiles (Acts 10) in the early days of the Christian era is still doing so.

A man in Ireland, convicted of sin, was on the point of believing when the devil raised his often-repeated objection: "If you believe, you could not keep it. What about tomorrow?" The worker dealing with him pointed to a water mill near by. "What turns the wheel today?" "The stream." "What will turn the wheel tomorrow?" "The stream." "And the days after?" "The stream." The anxious man was led to see that there was abundant grace to save, keep, and meet all his need. This rich grace is available to Jew and Gentile continually.

Finally, you must see the imperative need for immediate action and decision.

THE IMPERATIVE NEED FOR IMMEDIATE ACTION AND DECISION

When God's way is not chosen, there will always be peril and failure and loss and perdition. The Bible puts it this way: *"What shall we say then? That Gentiles, who did not pursue righteousness, attained righteousness, even the righteousness which is by faith; but Israel, pursuing a law of righteousness, did not arrive at that law. Why? Because they did not pursue it by faith, but as though it were by works. They stumbled over the stumbling stone, just as it is written, 'Behold, I lay in Zion a stone of stumbling and a rock of offense: and he who believes in Him will not be disappointed'"* (Romans 9:30-33). The time allotted for decision is now. No other time is promised us. *"Behold, now is 'the acceptable time,' behold, now is 'the day of salvation'"* (2 Corinthians 6:2; also see Hebrews 3:7-8, 13, 15; 4:7). The pleadings of the Holy Spirit in your heart keep stressing, "Today! Today! Today!" What is done must be done now.

When Antiochus the Fourth of Syria was met by the Roman ambassadors, bringing the senate's word forbidding his war with Egypt, he fully expected to reply on the next day. Popilius Lunas straightway drew a circle around Antiochus in the sand, and said, "Decide now, before you step out of that circle." This brought him to decision at once; he gave up the war and returned to his capital. The message of high heaven concerning eternity is, "Decide now," for now is the only time we have. Yesterday is gone, and tomorrow is not promised us. We have only *now* to decide.

There is no instance in Scripture of an individual or nation being appointed an opportunity to receive Christ as Saviour in any other age or time, other than the one in which they live. Take your opportunity now! Believe and be saved!

Scripture Index

Subject Index

of Israel, 118
to privilege, 120
Elephantiasis, 50
Elihu, 59
Elijah, 99, 108, 143, 157
Eliphaz, 55
Elisha, 101
England, 131, 132
London, 132
Northampton, 132
Esau
first, 16
Idumaean, descendants of, 19
married daughter of Ishmael,
15
represents the flesh, 15
Eternal, 123, 192
Europe, 20, 27, 36, 41, 58
Eye, 39
apple of, 39-44
diseased, 141, 142
easily injured, 40-41
little boy of, 39
little daughter of, 39
painful when injured, 43, 44
place in the body, 42
protected, 40, 42, 43
Ezekiel, 33

Fascists, 20
Felix of Nola, 53
Fighting
Arabs and Israelis, 20-21
Six-Day War, 21
Syria, 21
Firstborn, 18
Flesh
represented by Ishmael, 15
represented by Esau, 15
Foreign missions, 75
France, 132, 133, 163

Gabriel, 37, 126, 127
Gaebelein, 138, 139
Galileo, 198

Gaza Strip, 21
Gentile, 28, 158, 218
Gentiles, 126, 128, 145, 156,
158, 171
fulness of, 159, 160
times of, 159, 160.
See also Nations
Germany, 130, 131
God, 169, 175, 182, 186
attributes of, 26, 52, 59, 60,
97, 102, 124, 139, 176, 177
blessing of, 71, 72
concerning Israel
choice of Israel, 58, 118, 124
gave law to Israel, 122
known by Israel, 86
love toward Israel, 97, 185
not cast off Israel, 105, 106
not finished with Israel, 165
of Israel, 75
protects Israel, 39-44, 65
suffers with Israel, 43, 44
treatment of Israel, 57, 158
keeps promises, 186, 187
manifest in flesh, 143
mysteries of, 111, 112
of the nations, 75
of Shem, 26
plan of, 161
promise to Ishmael, 17
prophesies the future, 33
revelation of, 111, 122
speaks to Job, 49
Tetragrammaton, 146
Glory, 35, 121, 219
Gospel, 15, 28, 94, 100, 150,
151, 199, 211
enemies of, 15, 20, 118
of God's grace, 138, 148, 169
of the kingdom, 128, 162, 187
propagation of, 213
to the Jew, 170, 200, 211-216
Grace, 115, 116, 138, 148, 169,
220
age of, 126
Great tribulation, 160-163, 166,
187
Griffith Thomas, W.H., 159